Environmental Chemistry

Alan Winfield

Series editor: Brian Ratcliff

CAMBRIDGE
UNIVERSITY PRESS

PUBLISHED BY THE PRESS SYNDICATE OF THE UNIVERSITY OF CAMBRIDGE
The Pitt Building, Trumpington Street, Cambridge, United Kingdom

CAMBRIDGE UNIVERSITY PRESS
The Edinburgh Building, Cambridge CB2 2RU, UK
40 West 20th Street, New York, NY 10011-4211, USA
10 Stamford Road, Oakleigh, VIC 3166, Australia
Ruiz de Alarcón 13, 28014 Madrid, Spain
Dock House, The Waterfront, Cape Town 8001,
South Africa

http://www.cambridge.org

First published 2000

Printed in the United Kingdom
at the University Press, Cambridge

Typeface Swift   *System* QuarkXPress®

*A catalogue record for this book is
available from the British Library*

ISBN 0 521 78720 3 paperback

Produced by Gecko Ltd, Bicester, Oxon

Front cover photographs: Pointed rock formations in
Cappadocia, Turkey/Peter Adams/Telegraph Colour
Library

Acknowledgements

Photographs
1.1, Images Colour Library; 1.5, Lionel Moss/Lifefile; 1.7, NASA; 1.8 top, Garden Matters Photographic Library; 1.8 middle, Steve Turner/Oxford Scientific Films Ltd Photo Library; 1.8 bottom, Steve Kaufman/Bruce Coleman Collection; 1.11, David Frazier/Science Photo Library; 1.18, courtesy of Johnson Matthey Catalytic Systems Division; 1.21, article by Anthony Browne, Environment Correspondent, in *The Observer*, Sunday, 14 November, 1999, © *The Observer*; 1.25, article by Paul Brown, Environment Correspondent, in *The Guardian*, 04 November, 1999, © *The Guardian*; 2.1a, Andy Tickle/Greenpeace/Environmental Images; 2.1b, 2.6, Mark N Boulton/Bruce Coleman Collection; 2.5, 3.1, Nick Hawkes/Ecoscene; 3.2, 3.3, 3.4, Andrew Lambert; 3.5, GeoScience Features Photo Library; 3.10, Martyn Chillmaid/Oxford Scientific Films Ltd Photo Library; 3.11, Ian Richards/Lifefile; 3.15, Natural History Museum Picture Library; 3.18, Dave Thompson/Lifefile; 3.20a, 3.20b, Nigel Caitlin/Holt Studios International Ltd; 3.21, Ben Osborne/Oxford Scientific Films Ltd Photo Library; 4.1, Amanda Gazidis/Greenpeace/Environmental Images; 4.2, G. Burns/Environmental Images

Picture research: Maureen Cowdroy

Diagrams
1.12, courtesy of Dr J.E. Fergusson, University of Canterbury, New Zealand; 1.13, Finlayson-Pitts, B.J. and Pitts Jnr, J.N., *Atmospheric Chemistry*, John Wiley, Chichester; 1.14, reproduced by permission from Harrison, R. M., (ed.), *Understanding Our Environment*, Royal Society of Chemistry, Cambridge, 1992; 1.16, 1.17, 1.19, 1.20, courtesy Johnson Matthey Catalytic Systems Division; 2.7, Anglian Water plc; 3.22, *Chemical Storylines*, Heinemann, 1994

Tables
1.1, 4.3, *Digest of Environmental Statistics No. 20 1998*, Department of the Environment, Transport and the Regions, HMSO, London; 1.2, 1.3, 1.5, 3.3, 4.2, 4.4, courtesy of Dr J. E. Fergusson, University of Canterbury, New Zealand; 1.4, Bond, R.G. and Straub, C. P., *Handbook of Environmental Control*, 1, Chemical Rubber Co. Press, Cleveland, OH, USA; 1.6, 1.7, courtesy of Johnson Matthey Catalytic Systems Division; 1.8, data from UNEP website; 2.1, data from both Dr J. E. Fergusson and R. M. Harrison as above; 3.6, Fitzpatrick, E. A., *Soil Science*, Longman Group Ltd, 1986; 4.1, European Environment Agency, Copenhagen

Contents

Introduction

Cambridge Advanced Sciences

The *Cambridge Advanced Sciences* series has been developed to meet the demands of all the new AS and A level science examinations. In particular, it has been endorsed by OCR as providing complete coverage of their specifications. The AS material is presented as a single text for each of biology, chemistry and physics. Material for the A2 year comprises six books in each subject: one of core material and one for each option. Some material has been drawn from the existing *Cambridge Modular Sciences* books; however, the majority is entirely new.

During the development of this series, the opportunity has been taken to improve the design, and a complete and thorough new writing and editing process has been applied. Much more material is now presented in colour. Although the existing *Cambridge Modular Sciences* texts do cover some of the new specifications, the *Cambridge Advanced Sciences* books cover every OCR learning objective in detail. They are the key to success in the new AS and A level examinations.

OCR is one of the three unitary awarding bodies offering the full range of academic and vocational qualifications in the UK. For full details of the new specifications, please contact OCR:

OCR
1 Hills Rd
Cambridge CB1 2EU
Tel: 01223 553311

Environmental Chemistry – an A2 option text

Environmental Chemistry contains everything needed to cover the A2 option of the same name. It is divided into four chapters, corresponding to the modules The Atmosphere, The Hydrosphere, The Lithosphere and Treatment of Waste.

The book is shorter than the first edition, previously available in the *Cambridge Modular Sciences* series, as the A2 Chemistry options are now only half a term long.

The text, illustrations and data have been revised throughout to ensure accuracy and clarity and, for the first time, a glossary of terms is provided, linked via the index to the main content.

Author's introduction

The chemistry of our wider environment is a question of balance, that of complex inter-related systems which depend on each other. If we destroy this balance by our thoughtless interference, the consequences can be far-reaching. In this book we shall study the relationships between the chemical systems that occur naturally on our Earth, and the effects of human activity upon these systems. For the purposes of this study the environment has been divided into the atmosphere (the air), the hydrosphere (the water in rivers and oceans) and the lithosphere (the soil and rock of the Earth).

CHAPTER 1

The atmosphere

By the end of this chapter you should be able to:

1 describe the structure of the atmosphere and understand the terms *troposphere* and *stratosphere*;

2 describe the composition and temperature variations within the troposphere and stratosphere;

3 use the carbon cycle to explain the factors affecting the concentration of carbon dioxide in the troposphere;

4 explain the cycle of ozone formation and destruction in the stratosphere;

5 explain the role of ozone in the absorption of ultraviolet radiation;

6 describe and explain the effects of CFCs on ozone levels in the stratosphere;

7 discuss possible alternatives to the use of CFCs;

8 discuss the role of nitrogen oxides in pollution of the troposphere and their effect on ozone levels in the stratosphere;

9 discuss pollution effects of the internal combustion engine and the use of catalytic converters;

10 discuss the 'greenhouse effect' and the contribution made to this by carbon dioxide and other gases.

The Earth's atmosphere is essential for life (*figure 1.1*). Oxygen is required for respiration by animals and plants, carbon dioxide is needed for photosynthesis, nitrogen is used for making proteins, and ozone protects us from the Sun's harmful rays.

It has not always been this way. Five billion (5 000 000 000) years ago the atmosphere consisted primarily of water vapour, carbon dioxide and nitrogen. At this time the Earth was cooling, and heavy rains washed out most of the carbon dioxide. Around three billion years ago simple cells evolved into organisms capable of photo-synthesis. This produced oxygen, which has built up to create the atmosphere as we know it today. Part of the oxygen was changed into ozone by the Sun's radiation. Thus the conditions were created for the huge diversity of life now present on the Earth's surface.

● **Figure 1.1** View of the Earth from space.

The atmosphere extends roughly 2000 km above the Earth's surface and becomes less dense the higher you go. To study it, we divide it into four regions. These are the **troposphere** (nearest to the Earth's surface), the **stratosphere**, the **mesosphere** and the **thermosphere** (furthest from the Earth's surface). Only the troposphere and the stratosphere need concern us here.

Figure 1.2 shows how the temperature of the atmosphere varies with increasing height from the Earth's surface. You can see that at first there is a decrease in the temperature of the atmosphere, up to a height of approximately 15 km. This region is the troposphere. After this the temperature increases up to a height of 60 km. This region is the stratosphere. The change from decreasing temperature to increasing temperature is a temperature inversion and the height at which this change occurs is called the **tropopause**. (It can be seen that other temperature inversions occur at 60 km and 90 km.)

The troposphere

The troposphere contains 90% of the molecules in the atmosphere and extends from the Earth's surface up to between 10 km and 16 km, depending on the latitude. The temperature at the top of the troposphere is around 200 K (*figure 1.2*).

Mixing of different chemicals in this region is fast and this layer contains our familiar weather patterns. The dry atmosphere at sea level contains 78.09% nitrogen, 20.94% oxygen, 0.93% argon, 0.03% carbon dioxide and traces of other gases.

Important chemical reactions that take place in the troposphere include photosynthesis, respiration and nitrogen fixation.

The stratosphere

The stratosphere extends from 10–16 km to 60 km above the Earth's surface. The temperature of the stratosphere rises from just above 200 K at 12 km to 290 K at 60 km (*figure 1.2*).

The stratosphere contains nitrogen, oxygen (O_2), ozone (O_3), and some water vapour. These chemical species are active because radiation acts upon them, producing chemical changes. These sorts of changes are **photochemical** (see the box on page 7).

The radiation principally responsible for chemical reactions in the stratosphere is ultraviolet radiation from the Sun with wavelengths between 190 nm and 340 nm. For example, the production of ozone is brought about by ultraviolet radiation with wavelengths between 190 nm and 242 nm. Radiation with wavelengths below 190 nm is absorbed in the thermosphere before it reaches the stratosphere.

Chemical balance in the troposphere

The carbon cycle

The concentration of carbon dioxide in the troposphere depends on the various processes involved in the carbon cycle (*figure 1.3*). Carbon dioxide is removed from the atmosphere in photosynthesis:

$$CO_2(g) + H_2O(l) \longrightarrow [CH_2O](aq) + O_2(g) \qquad (1.1)$$

([CH_2O] is an empirical formula for a carbohydrate.)

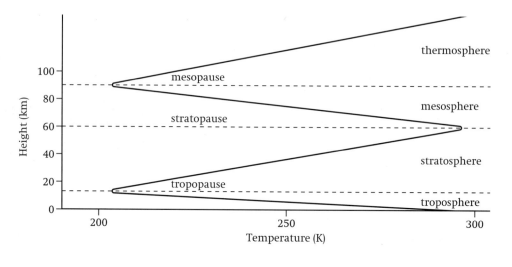

● **Figure 1.2** The variation of temperature with height from the Earth's surface.

Photosynthesis is carried out by green plants and is an energy-storing process.

Carbon dioxide is returned to the atmosphere by respiration in plants and animals:

$$[CH_2O](aq) + O_2(g) \longrightarrow CO_2(g) + H_2O(l) \qquad (1.2)$$

Respiration is an energy-liberating process.

Some carbon dioxide is also produced in the atmosphere by the oxidation of hydrocarbons, principally methane. This methane is given off by microorganisms in marshes and by animals, particularly ruminants, due to the micro-organisms in their intestines.

Atmospheric carbon dioxide is also in dynamic equilibrium with carbon dioxide dissolved in surface water. Dynamic equilibrium means that the concentrations of gaseous and aqueous (dissolved) carbon dioxide remain constant even though there is constant movement of individual molecules between the atmosphere and surface water:

$$CO_2(g) \rightleftharpoons CO_2(aq) \qquad (1.3)$$

Some carbon dioxide dissolved in the world's oceans is taken up by phytoplankton (minute plants and algae) in the process of photosynthesis. Some phytoplankton is eaten by fish and whales, and the carbon dioxide is then released back into the water in the process of respiration. Phytoplankton also respire at night, producing carbon dioxide.

The solubility of carbon dioxide in water under atmospheric conditions is $1.2 \times 10^{-5} \, mol \, dm^{-3}$ at 298 K and 1 atmosphere total pressure. Increasing the pressure increases the solubility, but increasing the temperature reduces the solubility (see chapter 2, page 28).

Cold surface water found in oceans at northerly latitudes, for example in the Norwegian Sea and off southern Greenland, has a higher density than warmer water and so this surface water sinks rapidly to great depths, taking dissolved carbon dioxide with it. When a chemical species is removed from the atmosphere by some means like this, the place where it ends up is called an **atmospheric sink**. Hence the cold oceans are an important sink for the removal of atmospheric carbon dioxide.

Dissolved carbon dioxide reacts further with water and establishes dynamic equilibria that are discussed in more detail in chapter 2:

$$CO_2(aq) + H_2O(l) \rightleftharpoons H^+(aq) + HCO_3^-(aq) \qquad (1.4)$$

$$HCO_3^-(aq) \rightleftharpoons H^+(aq) + CO_3^{2-}(aq) \qquad (1.5)$$

These equilibria result in a solution of carbon dioxide being weakly acidic, with a pH of about 5.6.

In general, the concentrations of carbon are in balance in the different sections of the cycle, but variations in the carbon dioxide content of the air do occur: there is more carbon dioxide at night and in the winter. Carbon dioxide concentration is increased by the combustion of fossil fuels and the removal of large areas of tropical rainforest, where photosynthesis is particularly rapid. This is discussed further on pages 4 and 22–25.

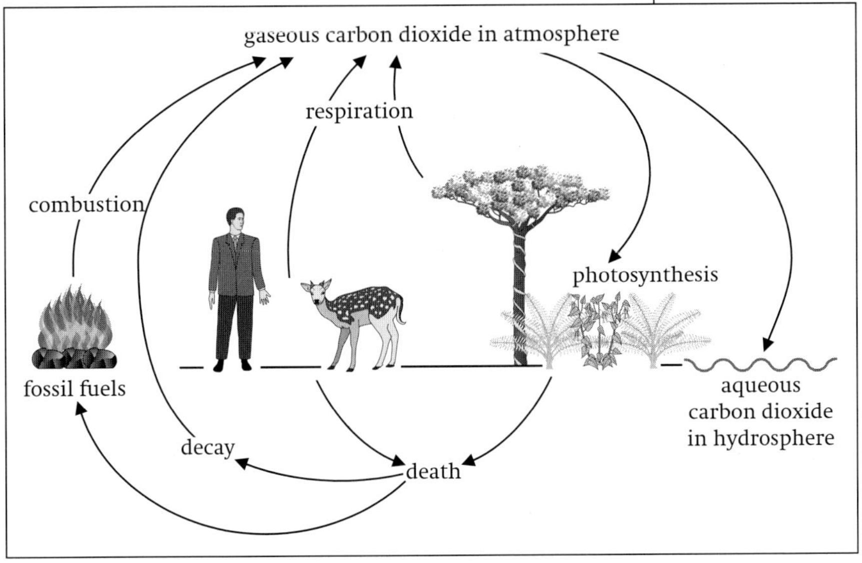

SAQ 1.1
Explain why carbon dioxide levels in the air increase in winter, compared to summer, and at night, compared to daytime.

Photosynthesis

As discussed above, the process of photosynthesis plays a key part within the carbon cycle in maintaining a constant concentration of carbon dioxide in the atmosphere.

● **Figure 1.3** The carbon cycle.

During photosynthesis green plants convert carbon dioxide and water into oxygen and sugars such as glucose:

$$6CO_2(g) + 6H_2O(l) \xrightarrow[\text{chlorophyll}]{\text{sunlight, } hf} C_6H_{12}O_6(aq) + 6O_2(g);$$
$$\Delta H = +2820 \text{ kJ mol}^{-1}$$
$$(1.6)$$

(The energy of radiation is given by the equation $E = hf$, where E = energy, h = the Planck constant and f = frequency of radiation, so the symbol hf is often used to represent radiation in chemical equations. See box on page 7.)

Photosynthesis is one of the most important processes in the world because it harnesses the energy of the Sun; some of this energy has been transformed into the chemical energy of fossil fuels. The energy of these is in turn converted to heat energy when the fuels are burnt, and the energy is then converted to electrical energy via the turbines of a power station, for use in homes, offices, industry and transport. Photosynthesis is also essential for the formation of agricultural products such as food, oils, forestry products, and organic and inorganic chemicals (*figure 1.4*).

The solar energy collectors in plants are mainly green chlorophylls, which are complex nitrogen-based organic chemicals with magnesium at their centre.

Most solar energy is captured at wavelengths of around 660–680 nm (red light) and 425 nm (blue light). Energy of around 430 nm is also absorbed, to protect the plant from radiation damage and for use in photosynthesis. The absorption of light from the visible spectrum at these wavelengths leaves the plant looking green.

A more detailed mechanism for *reaction 1.6* can be explained in the following terms.

■ Solar energy is used in the so-called 'light' reaction to decompose water to provide electrons:

$$2H_2O(l) \xrightarrow{\text{sunlight, } hf} O_2(g) + 4H^+(aq) + 4e^- \qquad (1.7)$$

■ The conversion of carbon dioxide into carbohydrates is a 'dark' reaction, not requiring solar energy:

$$CO_2(g) + 4H^+(aq) + 4e^- \longrightarrow \underset{\text{carbohydrate}}{[CH_2O](aq)} + H_2O(l) \qquad (1.8)$$

■ Respiration in animals and plants involves the oxidation of these carbohydrates, the release of their stored energy and the return of carbon dioxide to the atmosphere:

$$\underset{\text{carbohydrate}}{[CH_2O](aq)} + O_2(g) \longrightarrow CO_2(g) + H_2O(g) \qquad (1.9)$$

The destruction of rainforests (*figure 1.5*) may disturb this balance of reactions by removing substantial numbers of plants that would otherwise be carrying out *reactions 1.7* and *1.8*.

● **Figure 1.5** Rainforest in Kota Kinabalu National Park, Malaysia. The warm and humid conditions in tropical rainforests encourage rapid photosynthesis.

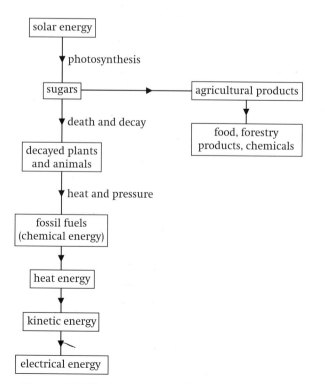

● **Figure 1.4** The importance of photosynthesis.

SAQ 1.2

Which areas of the visible spectrum does chlorophyll
a absorb
b reflect?

SAQ 1.3

Suggest how farmers can modify the conditions in a greenhouse to produce lettuces throughout the year.

SAQ 1.4

Predict how the destruction of large areas of tropical rainforest will affect the atmosphere.

Chemical balance in the stratosphere

Ozone

Ozone, O_3, is an important gas in the stratosphere. It is a form of oxygen with three oxygen atoms. It is produced in the stratosphere by the following photochemical reactions:

$$O_2(g) \xrightarrow{hf} O(g) + O^*(g) \tag{1.10}$$

$$O^*(g) + O_2(g) + M(g) \longrightarrow O_3(g) + M^*(g);$$
$$\text{ozone}$$
$$\Delta H = -100 \text{ kJ mol}^{-1} \tag{1.11}$$

M is a third chemical species required to take away excess energy. In the atmosphere this is usually molecular nitrogen and oxygen. An asterisk (*) is used to indicate energy-rich atoms or molecules. Thus in *reaction 1.10* solar radiation produces energy-rich oxygen atoms, sometimes called 'excited' oxygen atoms. In *reaction 1.11* M carries off excess energy as M^*.

The ozone produced in *reaction 1.11* absorbs ultraviolet radiation with wavelengths in the range 230 nm to 340 nm to re-form diatomic oxygen. The peak absorption is at 295 nm. The two reactions are:

$$O_3(g) \xrightarrow{hf} O_2(g) + O^*(g) \tag{1.12}$$

followed by

$$O_3(g) + O^*(g) \longrightarrow 2O_2(g); \Delta H = -390 \text{ kJ mol}^{-1} \tag{1.13}$$

You can see from *reactions 1.10–1.13* that ozone is being made and destroyed all the time. Over millions of years a state of equilibrium has been reached in which the rate of formation of ozone is equal to the rate of its destruction. Until very recently the thickness of the ozone layer in the stratosphere remained relatively constant. The situation has altered over the last 50 years as a result of chemicals released into the atmosphere (see pages 6–9).

You will recall from *figure 1.2* that in the stratosphere the temperature increases with increasing distance from the Earth's surface. You can see that *reactions 1.11* and *1.13* produce a considerable amount of heat; it is these reactions that cause the increase in temperature in the stratosphere. (The reactions are more likely to occur at higher levels because there is more ultraviolet radiation.)

It is the absorption of ultraviolet radiation in the stratosphere which prevents most of the radiation of wavelengths less than 340 nm from reaching the Earth. In this way, plants and animals are protected from this damaging radiation.

There are other reactions which remove ozone. The most important of these are radical reactions (box on page 6) with oxides of nitrogen, which occur at a height of roughly 25 km:

$$NO \cdot (g) + O_3(g) \longrightarrow NO_2 \cdot (g) + O_2(g);$$
$$\Delta H = -200 \text{ kJ mol}^{-1} \tag{1.14}$$

$$NO_2 \cdot (g) + O(g) \longrightarrow NO \cdot (g) + O_2(g);$$
$$\Delta H = -192 \text{ kJ mol}^{-1} \tag{1.15}$$

$$NO_2 \cdot (g) \xrightarrow{hf} NO \cdot (g) + O(g) \tag{1.16}$$

The dot (·) after a formula refers to the unpaired electron in a **radical**. The term 'radical' is used instead of the older term 'free radical'. Note that the oxygen atom is recycled and nitrogen monoxide, $NO \cdot$, is regenerated. This means that one molecule of a nitrogen oxide can remove many ozone molecules.

Oxides of nitrogen enter the atmosphere from biological activity and they can also be formed during the combustion of fossil fuels. Note that nitrogen monoxide does not rise into the stratosphere directly, because it is too reactive. The nitrogen monoxide in the stratosphere comes from

---

Radical reactions

Reactions in the upper atmosphere (stratosphere, mesosphere and thermosphere) are mainly radical reactions initiated by the strong ultraviolet radiation provided by the Sun. **Radicals** are reactive atoms or molecules with an unpaired electron. The reactions are chain processes that proceed by three stages. (All the reactions discussed in this box occur in the gaseous state.)

In the first stage, radicals are produced by the action of ultraviolet radiation. This is called the **chain initiation** stage. Initiation reactions in the upper atmosphere are:

$$O_2 \xrightarrow{hf} O + O^*$$

(O^* represents an energy-rich oxygen atom)

$$O_3 \xrightarrow{hf} O_2 + O^*$$

$$O^* + H_2O \xrightarrow{hf} 2HO\cdot$$

$$O^* + CH_4 \xrightarrow{hf} \cdot CH_3 + HO\cdot$$

Once radicals have been produced they can react with other molecules or atoms to produce further radicals, and a chain reaction is produced. This is known as the **chain propagation** stage. Propagation reactions are:

$$HO\cdot + O_3 \longrightarrow HO_2\cdot + O_2$$

$$HO_2\cdot + O \longrightarrow HO\cdot + O_2$$

$$HO\cdot + O \longrightarrow O_2 + H\cdot$$

$$H\cdot + O_3 \longrightarrow HO\cdot + O_2$$

Collision of radicals with each other removes these radicals. This is the **chain termination** stage. Termination reactions are:

$$NO_2\cdot + HO\cdot \longrightarrow HNO_3$$

$$HO_2\cdot + HO_2\cdot \longrightarrow H_2O_2 + O_2$$

·Note that the terms 'radical' and 'free radical' are synonymous. This book uses 'radical', as recommended by IUPAC, instead of the older term 'free radical'.

---

reaction of oxygen atoms with dinitrogen oxide, N_2O, which is unreactive in the troposphere:

$$N_2O(g) + O(g) \longrightarrow 2NO\cdot(g) \qquad (1.17)$$

Hydroxyl radicals, $HO\cdot$, are also involved in the removal of ozone. They are formed by the reaction of energy-rich oxygen atoms (from photochemical reactions) with water vapour:

$$O^*(g) + H_2O(g) \longrightarrow 2HO\cdot(g) \qquad (1.18)$$

These hydroxyl radicals can react with oxygen atoms in a chain reaction (see box), producing further hydroxyl radicals:

$$HO\cdot(g) + O(g) \longrightarrow O_2(g) + H\cdot(g);$$
$$\Delta H = -64\,kJ\,mol^{-1} \qquad (1.19)$$

$$H\cdot(g) + O_3(g) \longrightarrow HO\cdot(g) + O_2(g);$$
$$\Delta H = -326\,kJ\,mol^{-1} \qquad (1.20)$$

Above 45 km (i.e. in the upper stratosphere) *reactions 1.19* and *1.20* play an important role in the removal of ozone.

SAQ 1.5

Explain why temperature increases with height in the stratosphere.

SAQ 1.6

State the reactions which **a** produce and **b** remove ozone in the stratosphere.

Damage to the ozone layer in the stratosphere

The inter-related reactions for the production and removal of ozone in the stratosphere, described above, ensured that the amount of ozone in the stratosphere was sufficient to protect the Earth from excessive ultraviolet radiation.

From the 1930s until the late 1980s, chemicals called CFCs (chlorofluorocarbons) were used extensively in aerosol cans, refrigerators, air-conditioning systems and the production of plastics. They seemed ideal for such purposes because of their lack of reactivity, low flammability and low toxicity. However, since the 1980s, there has been much concern about the effect of CFCs on the ozone in the stratosphere and this has led to a severe reduction in their use, except for approved specialised needs.

CFCs are unaffected by ultraviolet radiation in the troposphere, but they are susceptible to attack by ultraviolet radiation in the stratosphere, releasing chlorine radicals.

Chlorine radicals in the stratosphere react with methane to form hydrogen chloride, HCl, or with

Photochemistry

Photochemical reactions play an important role in atmospheric pollution. These reactions are brought about by the action of electromagnetic radiation on matter.

The energy of visible light and of ultraviolet radiation is similar to that of the average chemical bond. Thus if a species absorbs photons from this region of the electromagnetic spectrum, bond dissociation can occur. For example:

C–Cl (in a CFC);
$E = 340\,kJ\,mol^{-1}$

The speed of a wave (or photon) is related to its frequency and wavelength by:

speed, c = frequency, f × wavelength, λ

The Planck equation expresses the relationship between a particular frequency of radiation and the energy associated with it:

energy, E = constant, h
          × frequency, f

The constant h, the Planck constant, has a value of $6.63 \times 10^{-34}\,J\,s$.

Combining these two expressions gives:

$$\lambda = \frac{hc}{E}$$

For one mole of bonds we need to introduce the Avogadro constant, L:

$$\lambda = \frac{Lhc}{E}$$

$L = 6.02 \times 10^{23}\,mol^{-1}$, and the speed of electromagnetic radiation, $c = 3.00 \times 10^8\,m\,s^{-1}$.

Substituting these values in the above expression, the wavelength of electromagnetic radiation required to split the C–Cl bond is given by:

$$\lambda = \frac{Lhc}{E}$$
$$= \frac{6.02 \times 10^{23} \times 6.63 \times 10^{-34} \times 3.00 \times 10^8}{340 \times 10^3}$$
$$= 3.52 \times 10^{-7}\,m$$
$$= 352\,nm \text{ (in the ultraviolet region)}$$

Figure 1.6 shows the relationship between energy of a chemical bond (in $kJ\,mol^{-1}$) and wavelength of radiation (in nm).

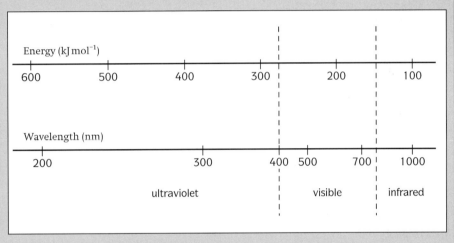

● **Figure 1.6** The relationship between energy and wavelength.

ozone to produce chlorine monoxide, ClO·. This chlorine monoxide then reacts with nitrogen monoxide, NO·, to form chlorine nitrate, ClNO₃. This is a natural cycle which has been occurring for hundreds of millions of years. The chlorine atoms in nature come from chloromethane, CH₃Cl, which is given off from seaweed, the oceans and burning wood. During this time a balance of ozone in the stratosphere has been maintained.

The problem now is the quantity of CFCs reaching the stratosphere and the length of time they remain there due to their unreactivity (see page 10). This leads to more ozone being destroyed than is created, as can be seen in the following reactions for two typical CFCs, CCl_2F_2 and CCl_3F. (All species are in the gaseous state.)

■ Initiation of ozone-destroying species:

$$CCl_2F_2 \xrightarrow{hf} \cdot CClF_2 + Cl\cdot \quad (1.21)$$

$$CCl_3F \xrightarrow{hf} \cdot CCl_2F + Cl\cdot \quad (1.22)$$

It is the C–Cl bond rather than the C–F bond which breaks because the bond enthalpy of the C–Cl bond, $340\,kJ\,mol^{-1}$, more closely corresponds to the energy of the ultraviolet radiation from the Sun (see box above).

■ Propagation:

$$Cl\cdot + O_3 \longrightarrow ClO\cdot + O_2 \quad (1.23)$$

The chlorine radical, Cl·, is regenerated by reaction with either oxygen atoms or nitrogen monoxide:

$$ClO\cdot + O \longrightarrow Cl\cdot + O_2 \quad (1.24)$$

$$ClO\cdot + NO\cdot \longrightarrow Cl\cdot + NO_2\cdot \quad (1.25)$$

This chlorine can then react with more ozone (reaction 1.23), this time leading to a loss of ozone without the absorption of radiation.

■ Termination of the cycle (M is some inert third body):

$$Cl\cdot + CH_4 \longrightarrow HCl + \cdot CH_3 \qquad (1.26)$$

$$Cl\cdot + H_2 \longrightarrow HCl + H\cdot \qquad (1.27)$$

$$ClO\cdot + NO_2\cdot + M \longrightarrow ClNO_3 + M \qquad (1.28)$$
$$\text{chlorine nitrate}$$

Reactions 1.26–1.28 remove the ozone-destroying chlorine radicals and chlorine monoxide species from the atmosphere, so they are called **atmospheric sinks**. The hydrogen chloride formed diffuses down to the troposphere, where it dissolves in water and is washed out in rain.

Chlorine nitrate cannot react with ozone, but it does undergo photolysis:

$$ClNO_3 \xrightarrow{hf} Cl\cdot + NO_3\cdot \qquad (1.29)$$

$$Cl\cdot + NO_3\cdot \longrightarrow ClO\cdot + NO_2\cdot \qquad (1.30)$$

$$ClO\cdot + NO_2\cdot \longrightarrow ClNO_2 + O \qquad (1.31)$$

Thus chlorine nitrate is only a temporary sink for chlorine atoms.

There is concern that these reactions are leading to a thinning of the ozone layer with the result that increased levels of ultraviolet radiation are reaching the Earth's surface. The consequences of ozone depletion in the stratosphere will be a cooling of the stratosphere and an increase in the temperature of the troposphere. Ironically this decrease in ozone levels in the stratosphere will lead to an increase in ozone levels in the troposphere (see page 16).

To predict the precise consequences requires three-dimensional atmospheric modelling on an enormous scale. Very powerful computers using programs of immense complexity are used to simulate possible atmospheric changes as a result of pollution. Monitoring the problem is made more difficult by natural changes in the ozone layer. The thickness of the layer varies with time and in space. Holes in the ozone layer come and go and levels are lower in winter and at night, due to lack of sunshine.

■ The British Antarctic Survey reported a 'hole' in the ozone layer over the Antarctic in 1985.

■ In the early 1990s levels of ozone depletion in the Arctic were found to be 50 times greater than scientists expected on the basis of atmospheric modelling predictions.

■ In the mid-latitudes of the Northern Hemisphere, the average ozone depletion has been 7% per decade since 1979.

The hole in the Antarctic ozone layer is caused by unusual conditions. Most ozone is created at the tropics and transported to the poles. Climatic conditions in the Antarctic winter effectively cut off a cone of air over the South Pole from the surrounding atmosphere. Air in this cone becomes very cold and clouds of ice crystals form in the stratosphere. Chlorine gas is released from chlorine nitrate:

$$HCl + ClNO_3(g) \longrightarrow HNO_3 + Cl_2(g) \qquad (1.32)$$
$$\text{in ice crystals} \qquad\qquad \text{in ice crystals}$$

When the air warms up and the Sun reappears in the Antarctic spring, different chemical reactions occur, the most important being:

$$Cl_2 \xrightarrow{hf} Cl\cdot + Cl\cdot \qquad (1.33)$$

$$ClNO_3 \xrightarrow{hf} Cl\cdot + \cdot NO_3 \qquad (1.34)$$

$$H\cdot + \cdot NO_3 \longrightarrow HNO_3 \qquad (1.35)$$
$$\text{absorbed by clouds}$$

Chlorine radicals react with ozone as mentioned previously (*reaction 1.23*).

The Antarctic hole was mapped using the Total Ozone Mapping Spectrometer (TOMS). TOMS was carried on the Nimbus–7 and Meteor–3 satellites between November 1978 and December 1994; during this time the ozone hole was discovered. The satellite 'Earth Probe' was launched on 2 July 1996 and now provides data on a near real-time basis (*figure 1.7*).

There are now controls over the manufacture and use of CFCs in the Montreal Protocol, agreed in 1987 and tightened further in 1990 and in 1997. Over 60 nations agreed to restrict the production and consumption of CFCs to 50% of 1986 levels by July 1998 with CFCs being totally phased out by 2000. In developed countries production had virtually ceased by the end of 1998, but a small amount of CFC production still continues in some developing countries. In the EU there has been no CFC production at all since 1995, although

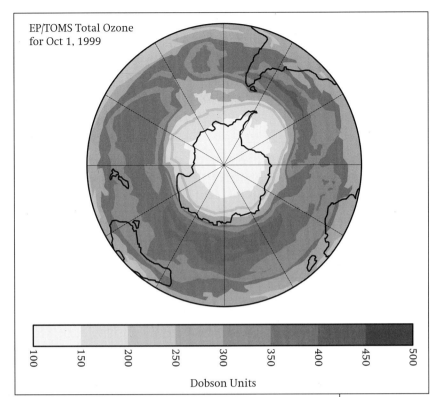

EP/TOMS Total Ozone for Oct 1, 1999

Dobson Units

100 150 200 250 300 350 400 450 500

- **Figure 1.7** Satellite map showing a severe depletion or 'hole' in the ozone layer over the Antarctic on October 1, 1999. The Antarctic ozone hole reaches a maximum in October each year, the Antarctic spring. Concern about the ozone layer in the Antarctic was growing in the early 1980s, with results being published in May 1985.

6000 tonnes a year are still consumed for 'essential' uses, as allowed under the Montreal Protocol, for laboratory and analytical use, and in measured inhalers.

World production of CFCs had decreased from a peak of 1 020 000 tonnes in 1988 to a level of 139 000 tonnes at the end of 1996.

Other halogen-containing carbon compounds that cause damage to the stratospheric ozone layer are tetrachloromethane, CCl_4, and bromomethane, CH_3Br. Large-scale production of tetrachloromethane has now ceased and there is international agreement to phase out the production of bromomethane by 2005.

CFCs remain unreacted for 50 to 80 years, so atmospheric modellers predict that it will take up to 100 years for existing CFCs to disperse. Meanwhile a search for substitutes is being made. The most likely candidates are the hydrofluorocarbons, HFCs, and hydrochlorofluorocarbons, HCFCs. These molecules contain C–H bonds, which are broken down in the troposphere. This initiates the breakdown of the entire molecule, with the result that the chlorine in HCFCs is unable to reach the stratosphere. Unfortunately both these types of compound are potent 'greenhouse gases' and may contribute to global warming (see page 22). The use of HFCs and HCFCs is therefore only a stopgap substitute for CFCs. It is planned to phase out the use of these substitutes by 2030 (2015 in the EU).

Effects of ozone depletion

Thinning of the ozone layer results in more ultraviolet radiation of wavelengths below 320 nm reaching the Earth's surface. Ultraviolet radiation in the wavelength range 290–320 nm is known as UV-B. In living tissue this is absorbed by nucleic acids and may affect genetic information, leading to increased levels of skin cancer in humans. Fair-skinned people are much more likely to develop skin cancers since they do not have the pigments that are present in dark skin that help to screen out the ultraviolet rays. Some predictions suggest that a 1% decrease in stratospheric ozone causes a 2% increase in UV-B and a 2–5% increase in levels of skin cancer. Another effect of UV-B is that it appears to prevent normal immune responses in the skin and other parts of the body. Large ozone depletions, and hence increased ultraviolet radiation, will also affect crop yields in plants due to cell damage.

Larvae of fish, shrimp and crab, zooplankton (tiny aquatic animals) and phytoplankton (microscopic aquatic plants) are particularly affected by ultraviolet radiation. Indeed, a significant increase in levels of ultraviolet radiation reaching the oceans could cause some microscopic life-forms to become extinct. Plankton are very important as they are the beginning of the food chain for all animals living in the sea. Phytoplankton take in carbon dioxide and give out oxygen into the water and into the atmosphere. Phytoplankton need only water, dissolved carbon dioxide, salts and sunlight to make all their vital substances. Zooplankton feed on these microscopic plants and are in turn eaten by fish. The fish are then eaten by other animals and humans. The effects of an upset in the ecological balance of plankton would be passed up the food chain and would be profound. Destruction of phytoplankton would also lead to more carbon dioxide in the atmosphere, and so would contribute to an increased greenhouse effect and global warming (see page 22).

SAQ 1.7

Give the property of CFCs which led to their original widespread use and now leads to their long-term presence in the stratosphere.

SAQ 1.8

Summarise in five equations the ways in which CFCs lead to the loss of ozone in the stratosphere.

SAQ 1.9

What are the types of chemical now being used as replacements for CFCs? Explain, chemically, why they do not have such a detrimental effect upon the ozone layer in the stratosphere. Discuss the disadvantages of their use.

Residence time

An important factor in the damage a pollutant can cause is the length of time it remains in the atmosphere. This can be expressed as the **residence time**.

The length of time a particular chemical is present in a given reservoir, for instance the atmosphere, is related to the rate of input of the chemical into the atmosphere from its sources and the rate of its removal to various sinks.

Think of a bath filling up with water. Water enters the bath from the tap – this is the source. Water leaves the bath down the plug hole – this is the sink. The bath is the reservoir. If the rate at which water enters from the tap is equal to the rate at which water is removed down the plug hole, the system is in equilibrium and the quantity of water in the bath remains constant.

The average time individual molecules of water remain in the bath is the residence time.

All non-permanent chemical species have sources, which put them into the atmosphere, and sinks which remove them, for example the oceans. Once molecules of a chemical species are in the atmosphere, the length of time they remain is expressed by the residence time.

The residence time (or lifetime) is given by the concentration of the given chemical species in the atmosphere divided by the rate of removal:

$$\text{residence time} = \frac{\text{concentration of given species}}{\text{rate of removal}}$$

We shall take the residence time as being the average time that a species exists in the atmosphere. Some residence times are given in *table 1.2* (page 12).

Atmospheric pollution

In December 1952 London was gripped by severe air pollution. In five days more than 4000 people died from its effects. Most of these were elderly or sufferers from chronic respiratory disease. Incidents such as this, and others like it, have alerted us to the folly of using the atmosphere as some kind of gaseous dustbin.

Fortunately air pollution of this intensity is now rare as a result of more stringent pollution control. Air pollution is now more insidious, less obvious in its immediate effects, but nevertheless can be equally as harmful over longer periods of time.

Emissions into the atmosphere are in the form of either gases or particulate material (*figure 1.8*). The term **particulate material** refers to dusts and liquid droplets in which the particles can have a wide range of sizes (10^{-8} to 10^{-4} m). Particulate material can also absorb gases.

Material emitted into the atmosphere is diluted with air and transported both vertically and horizontally. It also undergoes chemical and physical changes. Pollutants are either **primary**, emitted directly into the atmosphere, or **secondary**, formed in chemical reactions in the atmosphere.

Some emissions accumulate in the atmosphere, for example carbon dioxide. Others that are unreactive in the troposphere escape into the

Source	Black smoke	Sulphur dioxide	Nitrogen oxides	Carbon monoxide	Volatile organic compounds (excluding methane)
domestic	67	69	75	219	31
industrial	13	418	208	118	589
power stations	21	1318	449	178	5
refineries	3	123	47	6	2
road vehicles:					
petrol	14	12	546	3866	540
diesel	183	26	424	167	90
railways	–	2	20	11	7
other	38	60	291	80	847
total emission	339	2028	2060	4645	2111

● **Table 1.1** Estimated UK emission of primary pollutants for 1997, measured in thousands of tonnes.

● **Figure 1.8** Both human and natural activities cause pollutants to be emitted into the atmosphere.

stratosphere, where they participate in chemical reactions (for example CFCs, page 7).

There are a whole host of air pollutants, the main ones being the oxides of carbon, sulphur dioxide, oxides of nitrogen and ozone. All of them have damaging effects on human and animal health, vegetation and building materials.

Table 1.1 gives figures for emissions of pollutants into the atmosphere arising from human activity in the United Kingdom for 1997.

Temperature inversion

In the troposphere, air temperature normally decreases with height above the Earth's surface by about 1 °C for every 100 m of dry air. Sometimes the lowest layer of air is cooled by the ground beneath. This produces a temperature inversion, as shown in *figure 1.9*. Ground level emissions then become trapped in the stable inversion layer. Lowered wind speed prevents the mixing of air layers and the lower polluted layer thus becomes stagnant. At low temperatures fog may form. This adds to the problem by reflecting the Sun's rays and preventing the warming of the lower layer. Pollutants prevent complete evaporation of the water droplets in fog, thus making the situation worse.

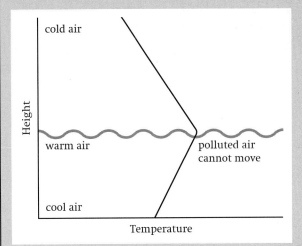

● **Figure 1.9** The temperature profile in an inversion. The height and temperature at which the inversion takes place vary with local conditions.

Material	Pollution sources	Natural sources	Residence time
carbon dioxide	combustion	biological decay	4 years
carbon monoxide	transport combustion	forest fires	1–4 months
hydrocarbons	transport combustion	biological processes	3–16 years
halogenocarbons	aerosols refrigerants	–	over 20 years
sulphur dioxide	combustion of fossil fuels	volcanoes	3–7 days
hydrogen sulphide	chemical industry	volcanoes biological processes	2 days
nitrogen oxides	combustion	biological processes	4 days
ammonia	waste treatment	biological decay	2 days
particulates	combustion	dust	varies

● **Table 1.2** The main gases emitted into the atmosphere and their sources.

Table 1.2 shows the sources of emissions on a global scale, both from natural sources and as a result of human activity.

Nitrogen oxides

The nitrogen oxides are serious pollutants. For example, they, together with hydrocarbons, are responsible for the photochemical air pollution that occurs in cities such as Los Angeles. Nitrogen oxides also contribute to the formation of acid rain. The main artificial sources of nitrogen oxide emissions in the UK are shown in *figure 1.10*.

Nitrogen can have a variety of oxidation numbers in its oxides:

NO_3^-, HNO_3	+5
$2NO_2 \rightleftharpoons N_2O_4$	+4
NO_2^-, HNO_2	+3
NO	+2
N_2O	+1

The main pollutant oxides nitrogen monoxide, NO, and nitrogen dioxide, NO_2, are frequently considered together, and are referred to as NO_x.

Nitrogen itself, N_2, has an oxidation number of 0. It is stable and has low reactivity. However, at high temperatures, such as in an internal combustion engine (see pages 13, 15, 18), it will combine with oxygen to form nitrogen monoxide:

$$N_2(g) + O_2(g) \rightleftharpoons 2NO\cdot(g); \Delta H = +180 \text{ kJ mol}^{-1} \quad (1.36)$$

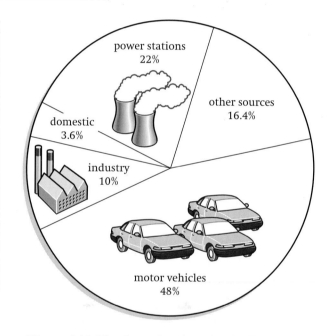

● **Figure 1.10** Pie chart showing the artificial sources of nitrogen oxides emissions into the atmosphere. Data from the UK, 1997.

At 298 K, K_p for *reaction 1.36* is 4.2×10^{-31}, showing the position of equilibrium to be strongly to the left:

$$K_p = \frac{p(NO)^2}{p(N_2) \times p(O_2)}$$

The partial pressures corresponding to the amounts of oxygen and nitrogen in the atmosphere are $p(N_2) = 81$ kPa and $p(O_2) = 20.3$ kPa, so, by substitution in the above expression for K_p, the partial pressure of nitrogen monoxide at 298 K is 2.63×10^{-14} kPa.

At the high temperatures of the internal combustion engine, for example 2000 K at the point of ignition, K_p for *reaction 1.36* is 2.98×10^{-5} and so, by a similar calculation, the partial pressure of nitrogen monoxide at 2000 K is 0.23 kPa. Significantly more nitrogen monoxide is produced at 2000 K.

Exhaust gases cool rapidly, preventing decomposition of the nitrogen monoxide formed. Nitrogen monoxide is thus a primary pollutant in the troposphere.

Nitrogen dioxide is formed by reaction of nitrogen monoxide with oxygen. It is therefore a secondary pollutant:

$$2NO\cdot(g) + O_2(g) \longrightarrow 2NO_2\cdot(g) \qquad (1.37)$$

Two molecules of nitrogen dioxide join together (dimerise), particularly at lower temperatures:

$$2NO_2\cdot(g) \rightleftharpoons \underset{\text{dimer}}{N_2O_4(g)} \qquad (1.38)$$

Dinitrogen oxide, N_2O, is a greenhouse gas (see page 23). It is produced and consumed by biological processes in soil and water. The main artificial sources are fossil fuel combustion, use of nitrogenous fertilisers, biomass burning, and animal and human wastes. Artificial sources represent about 45% of the output to the atmosphere.

Nitrogen monoxide, NO, plays a part in the removal of ozone in the stratosphere – see *reactions 1.14–1.16* (page 5). The nitrogen monoxide is formed by the reaction of oxygen atoms and dinitrogen oxide (*reaction 1.17*) and so is a secondary pollutant in the stratosphere.

Nitrogen monoxide in the stratosphere also plays a part in the destruction of the ozone layer by chlorine radicals – see *reaction 1.25* (page 7).

It has been estimated (1993) that annual emissions of nitrogen oxides are 53 million tonnes from artificial sources and 1092 million tonnes from natural sources. You can see that larger amounts of nitrogen oxides come from natural processes, for example biological activity in soil, volcanoes and lightning, than come from human activities. The problem with artificial emissions is that they are concentrated in urban areas and can reach high concentrations. The biggest source is the combustion of oil and petrol, followed by the combustion of coal. Power stations and transport are by far the biggest contributors to artificial nitrogen oxide pollution. Urban levels follow seasonal variations: the concentration of nitrogen oxides is significantly higher in winter. Over a 24-hour period, high concentrations of nitrogen oxides coincide with the morning and evening traffic peaks.

Photochemical smog

Photochemical smog is a whitish yellow haze containing chemical species which irritate the respiratory tract, causing long-term health effects (*table 1.3*, overleaf).

The chemical pollutants in photochemical smog are nitrogen monoxide, nitrogen dioxide, hydrocarbons, peroxyethanoyl nitrate (PAN), ozone and aldehydes. Nitrogen monoxide and hydrocarbons are the primary pollutants.

The conditions needed to form photochemical smog are a particular combination of atmospheric pollutants, sunlight, a stable temperature inversion (box on page 11) and land enclosed by hills. Such conditions occur in Los Angeles in the summer months (*figure 1.11*). In that city 68% of nitrogen oxide emissions arise from vehicle exhausts.

Figure 1.12 shows that the concentrations of the primary pollutants, nitrogen monoxide and hydrocarbons, rise during the early-morning rush hour. Nitrogen dioxide builds up as nitrogen

● **Figure 1.11** Photochemical smog in Los Angeles.

Subject	Pollutant	Effect	Concentration (ppmv)	Exposure time (hours)
humans	nitrogen dioxide	odour	1.0–3.0	
		death	500.0	48
	ozone	odour	0.005–0.05	
		irritation of throat	0.1	2
		shortness of breath	0.4–1.0	2
		irritation of eyes and nose	0.1	1
		impaired lung function, chest pains, coughing	1.5–2.0	2
		unconsciousness	11.0	0.25
		death	50.0	1
	PAN	reduced lung function	0.3	0.20
	HCHO	odour	0.1	
		severe distress	10.0–20.0	
plants	nitrogen dioxide	leaf lesions	2.5	4
		inhibits photosynthesis	0.6	
	ozone	leaf lesions, inhibits photosynthesis	0.1	2–4
	PAN	collapse of young cells	0.01	6
	HCHO	leaf symptoms	0.2	48
polymers	ozone	degradation and cracking of polymers containing double bonds (e.g. rubber)		

The concentrations of pollutants in this table are measured in parts per million by volume, ppmv. This means the number of particles of the substance per million molecules of air.

● **Table 1.3** Effects of pollutants in photochemical smog.

monoxide is oxidised. Later, the concentration of nitrogen dioxide falls due to photolysis in a complex series of reactions, which leads to the formation of ozone, aldehydes and peroxy nitrates. Nitrous acid, HNO_2, and nitric acid, HNO_3, are formed by reaction of nitrogen oxides with water, and are removed by rain or by aerosol formation. Nitrogen oxides and hydrocarbons produced in the afternoon rush hour are removed by reaction with ozone, leading to a drop in ozone concentration. Ozone in the lower atmosphere is an extremely dangerous pollutant (see page 16); this must be distinguished from its beneficial role in the stratosphere (see page 5).

The formation of photochemical smog proceeds by several steps. You will see that these involve many radicals (see box on page 6), that is chemical species with an unpaired electron. Atmospheric radicals are species rarely encountered in laboratory chemistry. All the species discussed here are in the gaseous state.

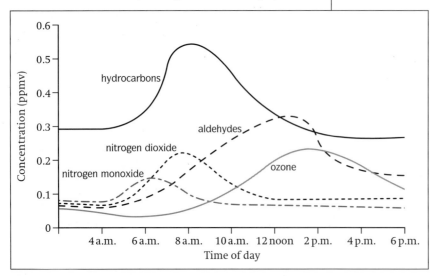

● **Figure 1.12** The variation in concentration of atmospheric pollutants during daylight hours in Los Angeles.

■ **Production of nitrogen monoxide**

This occurs at high temperature in internal combustion engines:

$$O_2 + M \rightleftharpoons O + O + M \tag{1.39}$$

$$N_2 + M \rightleftharpoons N\cdot + N\cdot + M \tag{1.40}$$

$$O + N_2 \rightleftharpoons NO\cdot + N\cdot \tag{1.41}$$

$$N\cdot + O_2 \rightleftharpoons NO\cdot + O \tag{1.42}$$

Reactions 1.39–1.42 may be summarised as:

$$N_2 + O_2 \rightleftharpoons 2NO\cdot \tag{1.43}$$

Further reactions are:

$$RH + O \longrightarrow R\cdot + HO\cdot \tag{1.44}$$

$$N\cdot + HO\cdot \longrightarrow NO\cdot + H\cdot \tag{1.45}$$

$$CO + HO\cdot \longrightarrow CO_2 + H\cdot \tag{1.46}$$

$$H\cdot + O_2 \longrightarrow HO\cdot + O$$

$$H\cdot + O_2 + M \longrightarrow HO_2\cdot + M \tag{1.47}$$

RH represents a hydrocarbon and R· a hydrocarbon radical.

You can see that hydroxyl radicals, HO·, play an important part in the formation of nitrogen monoxide.

■ **Production of nitrogen dioxide**

The direct oxidation of nitrogen monoxide to nitrogen dioxide,

$$2NO\cdot + O_2 \rightleftharpoons 2NO_2\cdot \tag{1.48}$$

is slow at atmospheric concentrations. An important reaction for oxidation of nitrogen monoxide is:

$$NO\cdot + HO_2\cdot \longrightarrow NO_2\cdot + HO\cdot \tag{1.49}$$

(The hydroperoxyl radical, $HO_2\cdot$, is a radical present in the atmosphere.)

The rapid conversion of nitrogen monoxide to nitrogen dioxide is explained by photochemical reactions involving ozone. Nitrogen dioxide is able to absorb radiation in the visible and ultraviolet regions ($\lambda < 400$ nm). This radiation breaks the N–O bond, which has a bond energy of 300 kJ mol^{-1} (*figure 1.6*, page 7):

$$NO_2\cdot \overset{hf}{\longrightarrow} NO\cdot + O \tag{1.50}$$

The oxygen atoms produced then react with diatomic oxygen in the presence of some third body, M, to form ozone:

$$O + O_2 + M \longrightarrow O_3 + M \tag{1.51}$$

M can be any gas molecule that is able to carry off the excess energy; in the atmosphere this is mainly molecular nitrogen and oxygen.

This ozone can then oxidise nitrogen monoxide to nitrogen dioxide:

$$NO\cdot + O_3 \longrightarrow NO_2\cdot + O_2 \tag{1.52}$$

Reactions 1.51 and *1.52* are both fast.

These reactions show that nitrogen dioxide is involved in both the formation and the destruction of ozone. The net result of this is an ozone level in photochemical smog in equilibrium with nitrogen monoxide and nitrogen dioxide, and dependent on the levels of solar radiation.

■ **Production of hydrocarbon radicals**

Hydrocarbons, RCH_3, in the atmosphere react with hydroxyl radicals, HO·, to produce hydrocarbon radicals, $RCH_2\cdot$:

$$RCH_3 + HO\cdot \longrightarrow RCH_2\cdot + H_2O \tag{1.53}$$

The radicals produced in *reaction 1.53* are very reactive and immediately become involved in other reactions. For example:

$$RCH_2\cdot + O_2 \longrightarrow RCH_2O_2\cdot \tag{1.54}$$
$$\text{a peroxyl radical}$$

Peroxyl radicals can oxidise nitrogen monoxide to nitrogen dioxide:

$$RCH_2O_2\cdot + NO\cdot \longrightarrow RCH_2O\cdot + NO_2\cdot \tag{1.55}$$

This alternative reaction for the oxidation of nitrogen monoxide reduces the need for ozone. The nitrogen dioxide produced in *reaction 1.55* can react photochemically by *reactions 1.50* and *1.51* to produce more ozone. The presence of hydrocarbons thus leads to the production of ozone. This has been shown to occur in smog chamber studies, where attempts are made to simulate atmospheric conditions in closed laboratory chambers.

■ **Production of aldehydes**

Aldehydes are formed by the reaction of $RCH_2O\cdot$ radicals with molecular oxygen:

$$RCH_2O\cdot + O_2 \longrightarrow RCHO + HO_2\cdot \tag{1.56}$$

You will remember that the hydroperoxyl

radical, $HO_2\cdot$, was also important in the oxidation of nitrogen monoxide (*reaction 1.49*).

Some of the aldehydes produced are oxidised to acyl radicals by the hydroxyl radical. For example, ethanal is oxidised to the ethanoyl radical:

$$CH_3CHO + HO\cdot \longrightarrow CH_3\underset{\overset{\|}{O}}{C}\cdot + H_2O \qquad (1.57)$$

■ Production of peroxy compounds

Peroxy compounds such as peroxyethanoyl nitrate (old name peroxyacetyl nitrate, PAN) have serious effects on health, irritating the respiratory system and the eyes.

PAN is formed from the reaction of ethanoyl radicals with oxygen and nitrogen dioxide:

$$\underset{\substack{\| \\ O \\ \text{ethanoyl radical}}}{CH_3C\cdot} + O_2 \longrightarrow \underset{\substack{\| \\ O \\ \text{peroxyethanoyl radical}}}{CH_3COO\cdot} \qquad (1.58)$$

$$\underset{\substack{\| \\ O}}{CH_3COO\cdot} + NO_2\cdot \longrightarrow \underset{\substack{\| \\ O \\ \text{peroxyethanoyl nitrate (PAN)}}}{CH_3COONO_2} \qquad (1.59)$$

PAN is thermally unstable and decomposes back into the peroxyethanoyl radical and nitrogen dioxide. The residence time (see page 10) of PAN is 14 days at $-10\,^{\circ}C$ and 8.6 hours at $+10\,^{\circ}C$.

The threshold for eye irritation is only 700 ppbv (parts per billion) for PAN and 5 ppbv for peroxybenzoyl nitrate, PBzN. Substances which irritate the eye in this way are said to be **lachrymatory**.

Reaction of ozone with alkenes in the atmosphere produces an aldehyde or a ketone and a peroxyl radical:

$$RCH{=}CH_2 + O_3 \longrightarrow RCHO + H_2\overset{+}{C}O\overset{-}{O}$$
or
$$RCH{=}CH_2 + O_3 \longrightarrow \overset{+}{R}CH\overset{-}{OO} + \underset{\text{methanal}}{H_2CO}$$

$$\overset{+}{R}CH\overset{-}{OO} + O_2 \longrightarrow \cdot OH + \underset{\substack{\| \\ O}}{RCOO\cdot} \qquad (1.60)$$

The peroxyl radical formed is thus available for further oxidation of nitrogen monoxide and for the formation of PAN (*reaction 1.59*).

Therefore we have a complex series of reactions in which the oxides of nitrogen and radicals play key parts. This complex series of inter-linked reactions is shown in *figure 1.13*.

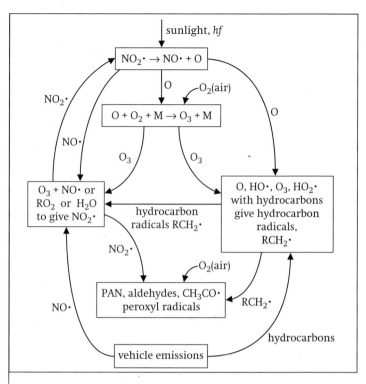

● **Figure 1.13** The chemical reactions that take place in photochemical smog are inter-related.

Ozone in the lower atmosphere

We saw earlier (page 5) that ozone in the stratosphere is essential in screening the Earth from dangerous ultraviolet radiation. In contrast, ozone present in the troposphere (low-level ozone) is a dangerous pollutant. Depending on concentration it can have a serious effect on human health, on vegetation and on synthetic polymers (*table 1.3*).

Ozone plays a part in the complex series of reactions involved in photochemical smog (page 15). The increased ozone concentration in the troposphere has arisen from photochemical reactions of primary pollutants originating from motor vehicle emissions and incomplete combustion of fossil fuels.

The natural background level of ozone near the ground is 20–50 ppbv. This ozone is present mainly as a result of transport of air from the stratosphere due to atmospheric mixing processes. Ozone levels above this background level are produced by reactions with nitrogen oxides:

$$2NO\cdot + O_2 \longrightarrow 2NO_2\cdot \qquad (1.61)$$

$$NO_2\cdot \overset{hf}{\longrightarrow} NO\cdot + O \qquad (1.62)$$

$$O + O_2 + M \longrightarrow O_3 + M \qquad (1.63)$$

$$NO\cdot + O_3 \longrightarrow NO_2\cdot + O_2 \qquad (1.64)$$

M is any gas molecule that is able to carry off the excess energy of the reaction. All species are in the gaseous state.

You can see that nitrogen oxides participate in both the formation and the destruction of ozone.

The fluctuation of ozone levels in urban areas varies over a 24-hour period. *Figure 1.12* on page 14 shows that the nitrogen monoxide produced from vehicle exhausts in the early-morning rush hour leads to a rise in the level of ozone via the formation of nitrogen dioxide.

SAQ 1.10

Explain in detail the variations shown in *figure 1.12*, relating them to *reactions 1.61–1.64* and to light levels.

Seasonal variations in tropospheric ozone in the Northern Hemisphere are shown in *figure 1.14*. High levels in June, July and August relate to longer hours of daylight and the greater intensity of sunshine.

Apart from the effects on health and vegetation mentioned in *table 1.3*, ozone in the troposphere has other detrimental economic effects.

- Ozone will add across unsaturated carbon–carbon bonds to produce breakdown products. Unsaturated carbon–carbon bonds are often found in synthetic materials such as plastics, paints and dyes. Rubber is a natural polymer containing carbon–carbon double bonds:

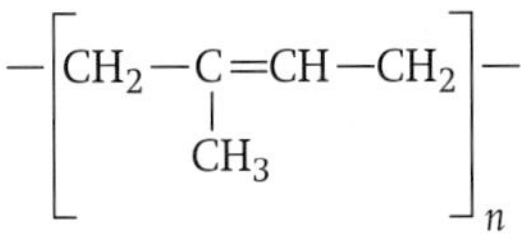

$$-\left[CH_2-\underset{\underset{CH_3}{|}}{C}=CH-CH_2\right]_n-$$

It is made from the monomer

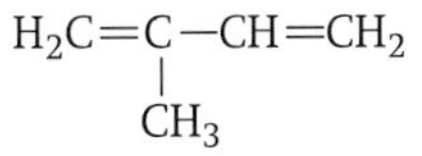

$$H_2C=\underset{\underset{CH_3}{|}}{C}-CH=CH_2$$

Ozone adds across the C=C bond to form an ozonide, which breaks down to give carbonyl groups:

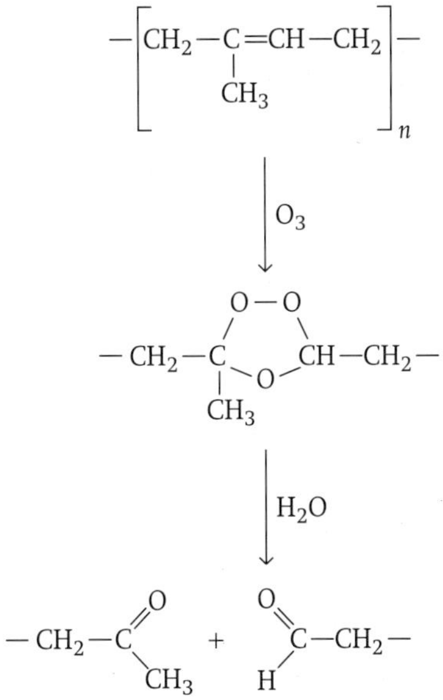

$$(1.65)$$

Reaction 1.65 causes rubber to crack, creating damage to car tyres.

- Ozone absorbs infrared radiation emitted at the Earth's surface, so tropospheric ozone contributes to the 'greenhouse effect' (see page 22). If the present tropospheric ozone level were to double, the average surface temperature of the Earth would increase by 1 °C.

SAQ 1.11

Give the systematic name of the rubber monomer.

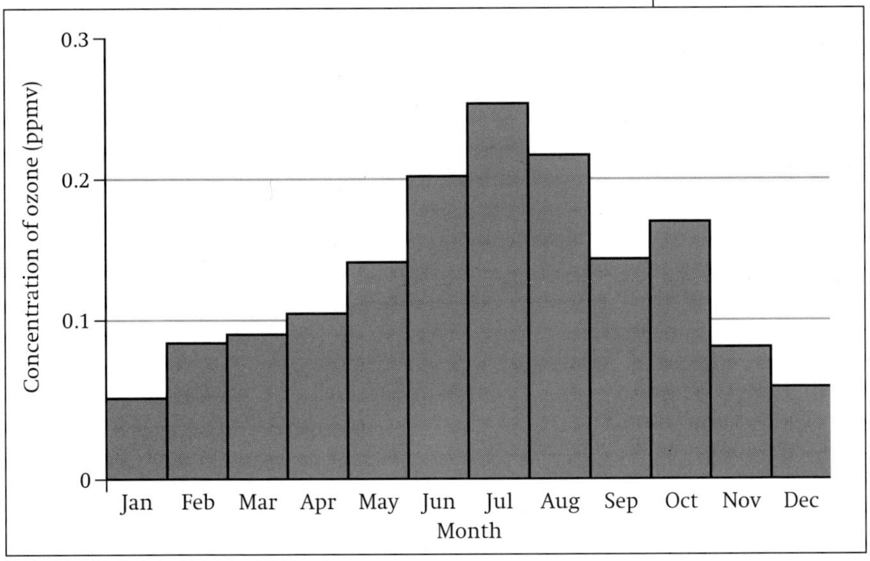

- **Figure 1.14** The seasonal variation in tropospheric ozone in the Northern Hemisphere.

Ozone levels in the troposphere down to 10 ppbv can be detected by the oxidation of potassium iodide followed by measurement of the concentration of iodine formed. Levels down to 1 ppbv can be detected by the chemiluminescent reaction of ozone with ethene.

The level at which tropospheric ozone is likely to cause damage to health has been defined in the US as exposure to a concentration of 120 ppbv for 1 hour. Levels in excess of this figure have been recorded in Britain during the summer months in urban, suburban and rural sites.

SAQ 1.12
a Ozone is a **secondary pollutant**. Explain what this means.

b Refer back to the reactions which lead to the formation of ozone in the troposphere and suggest methods for ozone control, giving chemical detail to your answer.

Pollution effects of the internal combustion engine

The motor vehicle has brought many benefits. Think of life without it! Unfortunately there is a price to pay in terms of atmospheric pollution.

Pollutants emitted from the exhaust manifold of an internal combustion engine are particulates, carbon monoxide, oxides of nitrogen, oxides of sulphur and unburnt hydrocarbons (*table 1.4*). Most of these pollutants are emitted from the exhaust. However, a significant amount of hydrocarbon pollution comes from the crankcase, carburettor (where fitted) and fuel tank, not from the exhaust. (In some parts of the world lead is still emitted from older cars that need to use leaded petrol, but in the UK leaded petrol has been unavailable since 1 January 2000 and has been substituted by lead replacement petrol, LRP.)

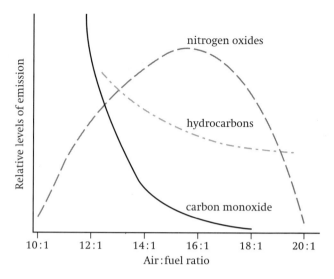

● **Figure 1.15** Exhaust emissions at various air:fuel ratios.

The engine draws a mixture of fuel and air into the combustion chamber, where it is ignited. The hot gases present after ignition are then expelled before a new charge of fuel and air is introduced. In the petrol engine ignition may be initiated by a sparking plug. In the diesel engine the mixture ignites spontaneously on injection into hot compressed air.

The air:fuel ratio plays an important part in determining the relative levels of emissions (*figure 1.15*). The most common ratios used are between 12:1 and 15:1 for petrol engines.

The stoichiometric ratio is 15:1. (Stoichiometric means the same ratio as in the chemical equation.) At this ratio it can be seen from *figure 1.15* that emissions of nitrogen oxides are relatively high, and emissions of carbon monoxide and hydrocarbons are relatively low.

To reduce nitrogen oxide emissions and to keep carbon monoxide and hydrocarbon emissions low, a high air:fuel ratio needs to be used. When there is more air than the stoichiometric ratio it is referred to as a 'lean' mixture. The trouble is that a lean mixture will lead to misfiring.

A richer mix (an air:fuel ratio lower than 15:1) reduces nitrogen oxide emissions but increases carbon monoxide and hydrocarbon emissions.

Let us study the relationship between the air:fuel ratio and

Fuel	Carbon monoxide	Hydrocarbons	Nitrogen oxides	Sulphur dioxide	Black smoke
petrol	236	25	29	0.9	0.6
diesel	10	17	59	3.8	18.0

● **Table 1.4** Emission factors for motor vehicles, measured in grams of pollutant produced per kilogram of fuel.

power obtained (*figure 1.16*). A balance has to be made between power produced, fuel consumed and pollutants emitted. You can see from *figure 1.16* that maximum power is obtained at an air:fuel ratio of about 12.5:1. *Figure 1.15* shows that this produces high carbon monoxide and hydrocarbon emissions and low nitrogen oxide emissions.

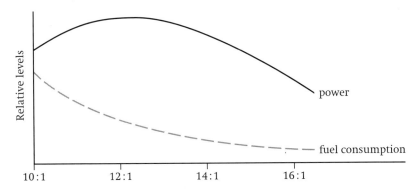

● **Figure 1.16** The relationship between air:fuel ratio, power production and fuel consumption.

Engine speed	Hydrocarbons (ppmv)	NO_x (ppmv)	CO (%)
cruise	200–800	1000–3000	1–7
idle	500–1000	10–15	4–9
accelerate	50–800	1000–4000	0–8
decelerate	3000–12 000	5–50	2–9

● **Table 1.5** Exhaust emissions and engine speed and load.

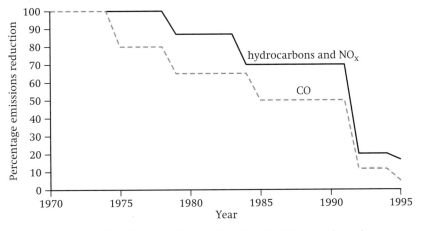

● **Figure 1.17** Reductions in allowed levels of pollutants in exhaust emissions; EU, 1970 onwards.

For lower fuel consumption an air:fuel ratio of 16:1 is needed, resulting in large amounts of nitrogen oxides and small amounts of carbon monoxide and hydrocarbons being emitted.

Modern engine technology has produced 'lean-burn' engines which use an air:fuel ratio of 18:1. These engines have specially designed combustion chambers and electronically controlled fuel injection to overcome the problem of misfiring.

Emissions also depend on engine speed and load, as shown in *table 1.5*. Acceleration produces the greatest emission of nitrogen oxides, whereas deceleration leads to high hydrocarbon and carbon monoxide levels in the exhaust gases.

Catalytic converters – a benefit of modern chemistry

By the application of careful research, chemists are enabling us to enjoy all the benefits of the car without the associated air pollution. Huge improvements in the reduction of harmful exhaust emissions are taking place, as is shown in *figure 1.17* for the EU.

Table 1.6 shows the progression of EU legislation on emissions from 1992 to 2005. The figures

	Date effective	Petrol			Diesel			
		CO	HC	NO_x	CO	HC + NO_x	NO_x	PM
Stage 1	1992	2.72	0.97		2.72	0.97		0.14
Stage 2	1996	2.2	0.5		1.0	0.9		0.10
Stage 3	2000	2.3	0.2	0.15	0.64	0.56	0.50	0.05
Stage 4	2005	1.0	0.1	0.08	0.5	0.30	0.25	0.025

The figures are in grams of pollutant per kilometre during a 20-minute test driving cycle.

● **Table 1.6** Development of EU emission legislation.

are in grams of pollutant per kilometre travelled and refer to a 20-minute test cycle on a rolling road (dynamometer). During this test cycle, the vehicle is driven according to a standard procedure which represents a typical European driving pattern.

SAQ 1.13

Calculate the reduction in grams of pollutant emitted per kilometre for hydrocarbons and nitrogen oxides (considered together) and for carbon monoxide that will take place between 1992 and 2005. Consider both petrol and diesel. Use data from *table 1.6*.

Exhaust emissions can be controlled by the use of catalytic converters fitted to exhaust systems (*figure 1.18*). Hot exhaust gases are passed over a mixture of platinum, rhodium and palladium on a supporting honeycomb structure of Cordierite ($2MgO.2Al_2O_3.5SiO_2$), which gives a very large surface area where the exhaust gases can come into contact with the catalyst. This is an example of transition metals being used in heterogeneous catalysis. Cordierite has a low coefficient of expansion, which is important for the stability of the catalyst surface at the widely varying temperatures of operation.

There are two forms of catalyst system – oxidation catalysts and three-way catalysts.

■ **Oxidation catalysts** can be used in conjunction with 'lean-burn' engines such as diesel to control carbon monoxide and hydrocarbon emissions. The exhaust gases of lean-burn engines are rich in oxygen. This enables unburnt hydrocarbons and carbon monoxide to be rapidly oxidised on the surface of the catalyst to give carbon dioxide and water at lower temperatures than normal (200–250 °C):

$$2CO(g) + O_2(g) \longrightarrow 2CO_2(g) \qquad (1.66)$$

$$C_8H_{18} + 12\tfrac{1}{2}O_2(g) \longrightarrow 8CO_2(g) + 9H_2O(g) \qquad (1.67)$$

Octane, C_8H_{18}, in the isomeric form 2,2,4-trimethylpentane is a major constituent of petrol.

Nitrogen oxides are not removed by this type of catalyst, but as you can see from *figure 1.15*, lean-burn engines have a low nitrogen oxide content in their exhausts. Tighter legislation has now made it necessary to control nitrogen oxide emissions as well.

■ **Three-way catalysts** work with conventional engines, controlling carbon monoxide, hydrocarbon and nitrogen oxide emissions. The nitrogen oxides are reduced to nitrogen:

$$2NO(g) + 2CO(g) \longrightarrow N_2(g) + 2CO_2(g) \qquad (1.68)$$

Palladium and platinum catalyse the oxidation of carbon monoxide and unburnt hydrocarbons. Rhodium catalyses the reduction of nitrogen monoxide to nitrogen.

Catalytic converters enable an air:fuel ratio of 15:1 to be used, with the pollutants being rapidly removed in the converter. If the mixture is richer than this there is not enough oxygen in the exhaust for the carbon monoxide and hydrocarbons to be completely oxidised. Cars fitted with three-way catalysts have oxygen sensors in their exhaust systems feeding back to the electronically controlled fuel injection units, so that the air:fuel ratio can be optimised.

The presence of rhodium in the catalyst enables it to start working at temperatures as low as 150 °C. Most engines attain an exhaust gas temperature of 200 °C or more within 30 seconds from a cold start, so the rhodium is an important factor in reducing emissions.

● **Figure 1.18** A typical catalytic converter, cut away to show the open honeycomb structure of the ceramic support coated with platinum, rhodium and palladium.

Catalytic converters have been installed in the majority of cars in the US since the late 1970s. In the EU all cars manufactured since January 1993 have had to be fitted with catalytic converters in order to comply with the law on tailpipe emissions. Catalytic converters are damaged by lead and hence can only be used in cars running on unleaded petrol. As mentioned earlier, leaded petrol was withdrawn from sale in the EU at the end of 1999.

Diesel exhaust emissions can now be controlled using a combined catalyst and filter system. The

CO	Hydrocarbons	NOₓ	Particulate material
2.0	0.6	5.0	0.10

Figures are grams of pollutant released per kilowatt-hour.

● **Table 1.7** Exhaust emission limits for heavy duty vehicles; EU, 2000.

principal harmful emissions in a diesel exhaust are carbon monoxide, hydrocarbons, nitrogen oxides and particulate matter. The particulate matter contains organic residues, including known cancer-causing chemicals such as benzo-α-pyrene, and soot, of which the most harmful kind is made of particles called PM10s. PM10s are very fine particles below 0.1 µm in size which can penetrate deeply into the lungs and have serious effects on health. Filter technology is now available to eliminate virtually all particles, across the entire size range. The EU exhaust emission limits for heavy duty vehicles manufactured from 2000 are given in *table 1.7*.

Figure 1.19 shows the actual, and projected future reduction in, carbon monoxide emissions in the UK resulting from the use of catalytic converters. You will notice that the projected reduction is roughly 6 000 000 tonnes by 2025.

Refer back to the section on photochemical smog (pages 13–16). *Figure 1.20* shows the enormous effect that the introduction of catalytic converters in the late 1970s has had on urban ozone levels in and around Los Angeles.

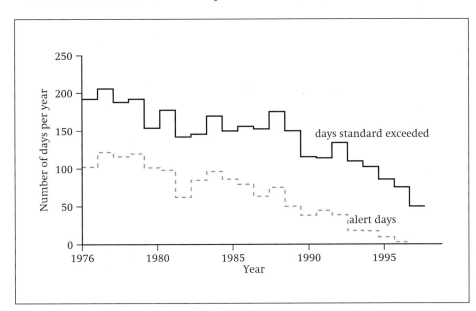

● **Figure 1.19** The savings, both actual and projected, in carbon monoxide emissions due to the use of catalytic converters; UK, 1970 onwards.

● **Figure 1.20** The number of days per year when photochemical smog, as measured by ozone levels, is a problem in Los Angeles has greatly reduced due to the use of catalytic converters.

The greenhouse effect and global warming

Look at the headline in *figure 1.21*. There is obvious concern about the rate at which the Earth's surface is heating up, and about the extreme weather events, such as hurricanes and cyclones, which have trebled in number over the last 30 years.

Climate depends on the global heat balance. A temperature change of 2–3 °C would have a pronounced effect on global and local climate. Of the energy which enters the Earth's atmosphere, 47% reaches the Earth's surface. Incoming energy from the Sun is in the ultraviolet, visible and infrared regions of the electromagnetic spectrum, with the maximum intensity at a wavelength of 483 nm – which is in the visible area of the spectrum. Because the surface of the Earth is at a much lower temperature than the Sun, the radiation re-emitted from the Earth is of lower energy and is in the infrared region (2000–40 000 nm), with maximum intensity at 10 000 nm. Some of this infrared radiation is absorbed by water vapour and carbon dioxide in the air and then re-emitted. The average temperature of the Earth's surface is maintained at 14 °C by the portion of this re-emitted radiation which is returned to Earth. If it was not for this re-emitted infrared radiation from water and carbon dioxide, the temperature of the Earth would be –20 °C to –40 °C at its surface. This method by which the Earth's surface is kept relatively warm is called the 'greenhouse effect', because it resembles the way in which greenhouses retain the Sun's warmth by internal reflection (*figure 1.22*).

The greenhouse effect creates a steady-state system in which the rate at which the Earth is absorbing energy is equal to the rate at which

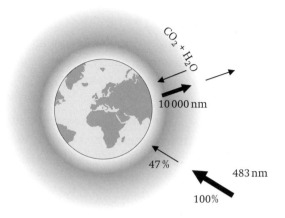

● **Figure 1.22** The 'greenhouse effect'. Some of the infrared radiation emitted by the Earth is absorbed by carbon dioxide, water vapour and other 'greenhouse gases' in the atmosphere. Some of this radiation is re-emitted back to the Earth, keeping the surface of the Earth relatively warm.

energy is being radiated back into space. This is a delicate balance which is being disturbed by emissions to the atmosphere. There is increasing concern that the rising levels of carbon dioxide in the atmosphere, together with other greenhouse gases discussed later, will lead to global warming with potentially disastrous climatic effects.

Levels of carbon dioxide in the atmosphere have shown a steady increase since around 1870. There are seasonal variations in carbon dioxide concentration and in the Northern Hemisphere it peaks in April and is at its lowest in September/October. This seasonal variation is in the most part caused by photosynthesis in the mid-latitude forests. Destruction of the rainforests could have a serious effect in raising the levels of carbon dioxide in the atmosphere.

As part of the International Geophysical Year in 1957, atmospheric monitoring stations were established at the South Pole and at Mauna Loa in Hawaii. Figures for carbon dioxide concentration

You've never had it so hot in 1,000 years

by Anthony Browne
Environment Correspondent

THIS YEAR is set to be the hottest of the millennium. With only six weeks

Office predicts December will be 'warmer than normal'.

The prediction is a dramatic reinforcement of evidence that the whole

Research unit at the University of East Anglia, a leading member of the intergovernmental Panel on Climate Change said: "There's a good chance

particularly shocking since this year has not had a notable heatwave. Not one month in 1999 has broken the record, but every month apart

and we had a sort of Indian summer.'

Met Office figures show that, up to 11 November, temperatures have been 1.25 degrees centigrade

● **Figure 1.21** Part of an article from the front page of *The Observer* newspaper 14 November 1999.

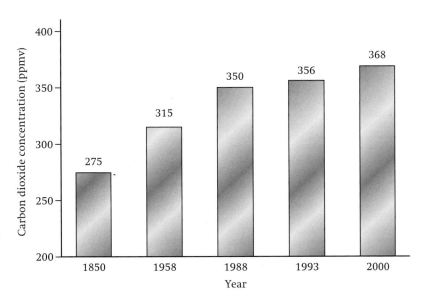

● **Figure 1.23** Carbon dioxide concentrations recorded at Mauna Loa, Hawaii, with earlier data from 1850 for comparison (see text for explanation).

from Mauna Loa are given in *figure 1.23*. The concentration of CO_2 is measured here in parts per million by volume, ppmv. This measure is frequently used where concentrations are very small. Here it is the number of particles of carbon dioxide per million molecules of air; 350 ppmv corresponds to a concentration of 0.035%.

How can we possibly know what the carbon dioxide concentration was in 1850, just over 100 years before the station at Mauna Loa was set up? This 1850 figure has been obtained very ingeniously from measurements on bubbles of ancient air trapped in the ice sheets of Antarctica and Greenland.

It is interesting to note the average annual rise in recent decades. In the 1960s the average annual rise in carbon dioxide concentration was 0.7 ppmv, in the 1970s it was 1.3 ppmv, in the 1980s it was 1.6 ppmv and in the 1990s it was 1.4 ppmv. The lower figure for the 1990s has been suggested to be due to the economic and industrial problems in the former Soviet Union during this decade. As mentioned earlier, there is a seasonal variation, which is about 7 ppmv at Mauna Loa.

Most of the carbon dioxide put into the atmosphere artificially comes from the burning of fossil fuels. However, natural sources have led to substantial rises in carbon dioxide levels in the past, long before the appearance of artificial sources.

Some molecules will absorb infrared energy because of the way their bonds vibrate. Molecules containing three or more atoms absorb strongly in the infrared region because of asymmetric vibrations that affect the dipole moment of the molecule. Bent triatomic molecules, such as water, have a permanent dipole and are able to absorb infrared radiation in both asymmetric and symmetric vibration and in stretching. There are several pollutant gases in the atmosphere that will absorb infrared radiation in this way. Gases which allow most of the Sun's ultraviolet and visible radiation in but prevent some of the Earth's infrared radiation leaving are called **greenhouse gases**. Apart from carbon dioxide, CO_2, and water, H_2O, other greenhouse gases include methane, CH_4, dinitrogen oxide, N_2O, CFCs and tropospheric ozone, O_3.

The greenhouse effect of a given gas is dependent both on its tropospheric concentration and its ability to absorb infrared radiation. The extent to which an atmospheric gas absorbs infrared radiation relative to the same amount of carbon dioxide is called its 'greenhouse factor'.

Gas	Greenhouse factor	Concentration in troposphere (ppmv)	Overall contribution (%)
CO_2	1	358	60
CH_4	30	1.7	15–20
N_2O	150	0.3	
O_3	2000	0.1 (varies)	20–25
CFCs	10 000–25 000	0.004	

● **Table 1.8** Greenhouse factors of various gases, relative to carbon dioxide, and their contribution to the 'enhanced' greenhouse effect – water vapour is not included.

Carbon dioxide is given a value of 1. The contribution of various gases to the greenhouse effect is shown in *table 1.8*. The more modes of bond vibration that are possible, the higher the absorption of infrared radiation.

From *table 1.8* you can see that some CFCs are 25 000 times more efficient at absorbing infrared radiation than carbon dioxide is. Fortunately their concentration in the troposphere is very low and is unlikely to increase because the production of CFCs in the developed world has now fallen to very low levels as a result of the Montreal Protocol and subsequent international agreements (page 8).

Closing the window

Carbon dioxide and water, the natural greenhouse gases, allow a certain amount of radiation to escape back into space through what is known as a 'radiation window'. Carbon dioxide absorbs infrared radiation with wavelengths between 12 500 nm and 17 000 nm. Water absorbs principally between 4500 nm and 7000 nm. In this way a 'window' is created between 7000 nm and 12 500 nm (*figure 1.24*). About 70% of the Earth's radiation is able to escape through this window, thus maintaining the ambient temperature of the Earth's surface.

The increased greenhouse effect, and hence global warming, caused by increases in carbon dioxide emissions to the troposphere has already been mentioned. Some other greenhouse gases which are not normally present in the atmosphere absorb radiation in the vital 'window' area of the infrared spectrum. For example, CFCs have a very large greenhouse factor partly due to their absorption of infrared radiation in this window.

Global warming

It has been predicted that the build-up of greenhouse gases in the troposphere will lead to an increase in the Earth's surface temperature. This is called **global warming**. The Earth's average temperature in 2000 was 1 °C above its 1850 value (1850 is chosen as the baseline as this precedes the polluting effects of the Industrial Revolution). The rise from 1970 to 2000 has been 0.4 °C. Comparing these values gives a feel for the accelerating rate of global warming. The average rise from 1850 to 1970 works out as 0.005 °C per year but for 1970 to 2000 the average rise is 0.013 °C per year, over twice the 1850–1970 value.

Making predictions is very difficult as it involves so many variable factors. Information is fed into very powerful computers which use mathematical models to predict climate changes.

Computer predictions produced in November 1999 by the Hadley Centre for Climate Change in the UK as a result of 5 years research suggest the climate may be heating up far faster than originally predicted. So fast, in fact, that natural systems would be unable to adapt and world food production would be affected. Higher temperatures would cause die-back in tropical rainforests and would increase microbe activity in soils. Most of the Amazon rainforest is predicted to disappear on this model due to die-back. Carbon in the wood would be released as carbon dioxide, putting millions of extra tonnes into the atmosphere. At the same time, the increased warmth of the soil would cause microbes to release more carbon dioxide.

In 1989, predictions of the rise in the Earth's average

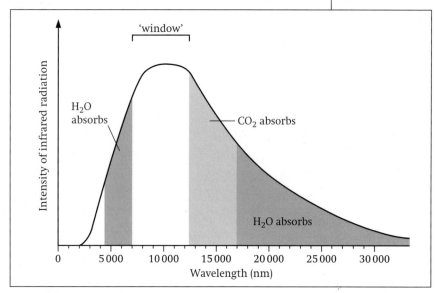

● **Figure 1.24** The Earth's infrared radiation spectrum, showing the 'window' between 7000 nm and 12 500 nm.

Century of natural disasters predicted

New study shows global warming is overwhelming nature's defences

Paul Brown
Environment Correspondent

The world's climate is heating up far faster than predicted, with the average temperatures in Europe soaring in the next century, according to new super-computer predictions.

The increase will be faster than at any time in the world's history. It will be far too fast for natural systems to adapt and will threaten world food production.

ging their feet over the last decade, the cuts proposed in carbon dioxide emissions are just not enough. It is going to hurt most the poorest people in the world, the subsistence farmers who will no longer be able feed themselves."

The computer modelling leader, Peter Cox, who had spent more than five years on the die-back of forest and release of carbon dioxide from soil, said the previous internationally accepted cal

● **Figure 1.25** Part of an article in *The Guardian* newspaper, 4 November 1999.

temperature due to build-up of greenhouse gases were between 1.5 and 2.5 °C by 2100, but the 1999 predictions suggested that the rise may be as much as 8 °C above the 1850 level by 2100 for land masses including Europe. Extreme weather events are already occurring more regularly (*figure 1.25*). The cuts in carbon dioxide emissions proposed by the Climate Change Convention are not enough to prevent the changes predicted.

Internationally accepted calculations had put the level of carbon dioxide in 2100 at twice its current value if no attempt was made to reduce emissions. The new research, which takes into account die-back of rainforests and increased soil microbe activity, now puts the 2100 value at three times the current value if there is no reduction in carbon dioxide emissions. It had been thought that increased levels of carbon dioxide in the atmosphere would increase forest growth because of increased photosynthesis, thus removing some

carbon dioxide from the atmosphere. However, the new research suggests that increased temperatures will increase respiration in the forests and lead to the die-back of healthy growth.

1999 figures show that of the greenhouse gases already in the atmosphere, carbon dioxide was responsible for over 60% of the 'enhanced' greenhouse effect, methane from past emissions was responsible for 15–20% and dinitrogen oxide, CFCs and ozone were responsible for the remaining 20%. In 1995, carbon dioxide accounted for 82% of total greenhouse gas emissions.

Between 1990 and 1998 there was a rise of 3.5% in greenhouse gas emissions from the world's richest countries (those in the OECD). Emissions from eastern Europe and the former Soviet Union declined by 28% over the same period, due to reduced economic activity. Overall the emissions from developed countries were down by 4.6% over the years 1990-98. Predictions for 1990–2000 were for a reduction of 3%. Worldwide, it is thought that the 2010 values for greenhouse gas emissions will be 8% above the 1990 values, with the increase the result of population growth and increased economic activity.

Clearly the predicted problem of global warming needs to be tackled urgently if there are not to be profoundly adverse effects on agriculture, sea levels, ecosystems, water resources, human health and weather.

SAQ 1.14
The United Nations Environment Project, UNEP, states in its July 1999 report that if no new policies are adopted to reduce carbon dioxide emissions, the amount of fuel burnt will rise from 7 billion tonnes of carbon per year in 1990 to 20 billion tonnes of carbon per year in 2100. What increase in mass of carbon dioxide will this release to the atmosphere? What assumption do you make in your calculation?

SAQ 1.15
Explain why the percentage increase in the concentration of carbon dioxide in the troposphere, as measured at the Mauna Loa laboratory, is actually less than the percentage increase in the concentration of carbon dioxide released to the troposphere from the burning of fossil fuels.

SUMMARY

◆ The troposphere extends from the Earth's surface to a height of about 15 km. In the troposphere the temperature decreases with distance from the Earth's surface.

◆ The stratosphere extends from about 15 km to 60 km above the Earth. In the stratosphere the temperature increases with distance from the Earth's surface.

◆ The concentration of carbon dioxide in the troposphere depends on photosynthesis, plant and animal respiration, the dissolving of carbon dioxide in surface waters and the quantity of carbon dioxide emitted during the combustion of fossil fuels.

◆ There is a natural balance of ozone in the stratosphere as a result of photochemical reactions.

◆ Ozone is important in the stratosphere as it absorbs ultraviolet radiation from the Sun which would be harmful to plants and animals if it reached the Earth's surface.

◆ Reactions of chlorine radicals released from CFCs are destroying ozone in the stratosphere.

◆ HFCs and HCFCs are temporary replacements for CFCs.

◆ Nitrogen oxides from fossil fuel combustion are major pollutants.

◆ Nitrogen monoxide influences the balance between ozone and oxygen in the stratosphere.

◆ Photochemical smog is a complex mixture of nitrogen oxides, hydrocarbons, PAN, ozone and aldehydes. Nitrogen monoxide and hydrocarbons are the primary pollutants.

◆ Photochemical smog has detrimental effects on human, animal and plant health. It contributes to the deterioration of polymers.

◆ Catalytic converters are an effective way of reducing harmful emissions from motor vehicles.

◆ The 'greenhouse effect' is a natural phenomenon which keeps the Earth's surface warm.

◆ Increased emissions of carbon dioxide, methane, CFCs and other gases are enhancing the 'greenhouse effect' causing the Earth's surface to warm up – 'global warming'.

◆ The 'greenhouse effect' of a gas depends on its concentration in the atmosphere and its ability to absorb infrared radiation.

Questions

1 Explain the terms troposphere and stratosphere. Discuss and explain the variations in temperature with height above the Earth's surface up to 60 km (*figure 1.2*).

2 Discussions on the causes of global warming centre around additional emissions into the atmosphere caused by human activity.

   a Describe two important ways in which gases containing carbon are emitted into the atmosphere.

   b Name two emissions which contribute to global warming but which do not contain carbon.

   c Explain briefly how increased concentrations of carbon dioxide may contribute to global warming.

   d Give balanced equations for two chemical reactions by which carbon dioxide is removed from the atmosphere.

3 Los Angeles has, on average, a temperature inversion every other day.

   a What is meant by temperature inversion in this context?

   b What two harmful consequences follow from these temperature inversions and why?

   c Explain why these consequences are most apparent in the middle of the day, and not at peak traffic periods.

CHAPTER 2

The hydrosphere

By the end of this chapter you should be able to:

1 describe the effects of water temperature and gas pressure on the solubility of gases in water;

2 explain the natural acidity of rain-water due to carbon dioxide and the enhanced acidity due to the presence of soluble nitrogen and sulphur oxides;

3 describe and explain the importance of dissolved oxygen in the support of aquatic life and the decomposition of organic material;

4 explain the role of dissolved carbon dioxide in the formation of temporary hardness in water;

5 discuss the chemistry of methods for the removal of temporary hardness;

6 outline methods for the production of drinking water.

The waters of the Earth are essential to its functioning at all levels. From climate and geology to the minute cells of life, the presence of water plays a fundamental role in our environment. Water affects the world's weather patterns, it stores heat and transfers power, it forms the basis of the natural chemistry of the Earth, and life itself is dependent on the ready availability of water of good quality.

Chemistry at the water surface

Much of the chemistry of natural water and the life which it supports is dependent upon dissolved gases that cross the water surface.

At the water surface, or air–water interface, exchange of materials occurs between the atmosphere and the hydrosphere.

The amount of water vapour in the atmosphere is measured by relative humidity:

$$\text{relative humidity} = \frac{\text{quantity of water in the air at } t\,^{\circ}\text{C}}{\text{maximum quantity air can hold at } t\,^{\circ}\text{C}}$$

The equilibrium $H_2O(l) \rightleftharpoons H_2O(g)$ moves to the right with increasing temperature. Fortunately, due to the continual movement of the atmosphere, liquid–vapour equilibrium is rarely attained, otherwise the high humidities reached would make life uncomfortable. High humidity is unpleasant because the concentration of water molecules in the atmosphere makes it difficult for water to evaporate from the surface of the skin, so the process of sweating is impaired and the body cannot cool easily.

Solubility of gases

The solubility of gases in water is affected by the temperature of the water and the pressure of the gas in contact with it. The dissolving of gases is nearly always an exothermic process. Therefore, if the pressure remains constant, the solubility will decrease as the temperature increases. This is in accordance with Le Chatelier's principle.

Increasing the pressure of the gas in contact with the water surface will increase its solubility. There will be more molecules of gas in contact with the surface, therefore more will dissolve. This can be expressed more formally as Henry's law, which states that the mass of gas, m, dissolved by a given volume of solvent is directly proportional to the pressure of the gas, p, provided the temperature remains constant and there is no reaction between the gas and the solvent. This can be written as:

$$m = kp$$

where k is the Henry's law constant, which is different for each gas and is dependent upon temperature. Using Henry's law, the concentration of dissolved gases can be calculated, but this is beyond the scope of this book.

The water cycle

On the Earth's surface there are 1500 million cubic kilometres of water. Of this 98.3% is in the oceans and 1.6% is frozen as ice. The remainder is ground-water, with a small quantity in lakes and rivers. This water goes through a series of changes known as the **water cycle**.

Water passes into the atmosphere by evaporation from water surfaces and by transpiration from plants. When the water vapour reaches the cooler parts of the atmosphere it condenses to form clouds. The water then returns to the Earth's surface as rain or snow. About half of the rain that falls on land is returned to the atmosphere by evaporation and transpiration. The rest seeps through the soil and rocks, and flows by streams and rivers back to the sea.

The water in the cycle can dissolve or react with the various materials it comes into contact with.

Rain-water

Carbon dioxide dissolves in rain-water and reaches an equilibrium with carbon dioxide in the surrounding air:

$$CO_2(g) \rightleftharpoons CO_2(aq) \tag{2.1}$$

Some of the dissolved carbon dioxide reacts chemically with the water:

$$CO_2(aq) + H_2O(l) \rightleftharpoons H^+(aq) + HCO_3^-(aq) \tag{2.2}$$
$$\rightleftharpoons 2H^+(aq) + CO_3^{2-}(aq) \tag{2.3}$$

The presence of hydrogen ions makes rain-water acidic, with a pH of about 5.7.

Oxides of nitrogen and sulphur, both artificial and from natural sources, may also dissolve in the rain to produce nitric and sulphuric acid. For SO_2:

$$SO_2(g) + H_2O(l) \rightleftharpoons H_2SO_3(aq) \tag{2.4}$$
$$\rightleftharpoons H^+(aq) + HSO_3^-(aq) \tag{2.5}$$
$$\rightleftharpoons 2H^+(aq) + SO_3^{2-}(aq) \tag{2.6}$$

The $HSO_3^-(aq)$ can be oxidised:

$$HSO_3^-(aq) + H_2O(l) \longrightarrow HSO_4^-(aq) + 2H^+(aq) + 2e^- \tag{2.7}$$

Some of the hydrogen ions formed in these reactions are removed by reaction with oxygen:

$$O_2(g) + 4H^+(aq) + 4e^- \longrightarrow 2H_2O(l) \tag{2.8}$$

Nitrous acid, HNO_2, and nitric acid, HNO_3, are formed by the reaction of nitrogen oxides with water in a series of complex radical reactions. These may be summarised as:

$$2NO \cdot (g) + O_2(g) \rightleftharpoons 2NO_2 \cdot (g) \tag{2.9}$$
$$NO \cdot (g) + HO_2 \cdot (g) \longrightarrow NO_2 \cdot (g) + HO \cdot (g) \tag{2.10}$$
$$3NO_2 \cdot (g) + H_2O(l) \longrightarrow 2HNO_3(aq) + NO \cdot (g) \tag{2.11}$$

You will recall from chapter 1 (page 18) that artificial sources of nitrogen oxides in the atmosphere include emissions from vehicle exhausts. Sulphur oxides result from the combustion of fossil fuels. When these acidic oxides dissolve in rain-water they give it a pH value of between 5 and 6, although in 'acid rain' the pH may fall as low as 2.

Sulphur dioxide originating in the UK forms sulphuric acid aerosols that can be precipitated in Scandinavia, increasing the acidity of the lakes and destroying aquatic life. Acid rain also leaches nutrients from soils and enables many toxic metal ions to dissolve more readily in soil solution. These may then enter the food chain. Aluminium released into Scandinavian lakes is responsible for the death of fish. Acid rain increases the rate of corrosion of metals and buildings containing limestone or marble and affects the growth of trees (*figure 2.1*).

● **Figure 2.1**
a Spruce trees denuded by acid rain in the Czech Republic.
b A statue whose stone has been eroded by acid rain.

Rain-water will dissolve calcium carbonate-based rocks:

$$CaCO_3(s) + CO_2(aq) + H_2O(l) \longrightarrow Ca^{2+}(aq) + 2HCO_3^-(aq) \qquad (2.12)$$

and some silicate rocks:

$$Mg_2SiO_4(s) + 4H_2O(l) \longrightarrow 2Mg(OH)_2(aq) + Si(OH)_4(aq) \qquad (2.13)$$

$$Mg(OH)_2(aq) \rightleftharpoons Mg^{2+}(aq) + 2OH^-(aq) \qquad (2.14)$$

The resulting ions make the water slightly alkaline, pH 8, and are carried through the river system and into the oceans.

SAQ 2.1

Summarise the factors which lead to the acidity of rain–water. Give appropriate equations. Outline the detrimental effects of acid rain.

Natural waters

The dissolved species in typical samples of sea-water, river-water and rain-water are given in *table 2.1*. The composition of river-water can vary widely according to the types of rock that it, and its feeder streams, have passed over. Ions in the underlying rock will dissolve according to their solubility.

You can see that, although rivers run into the sea, there are pronounced differences between the composition of sea-water and that of river-water. It is interesting to note that the sodium ion, $Na^+(aq)$, is the most abundant metal ion in sea-water whereas the calcium ion, $Ca^{2+}(aq)$, is the most abundant in river-water. The reason for this is that the sodium ion has a very long residence time in the sea. A constant sodium ion balance is maintained by ion exchange with the clays in the sediment at the bottom of the sea:

$$Na^+(aq) + M-clay(s) \rightleftharpoons Na-clay(s) + M^+(aq) \qquad (2.15)$$

The notation M–clay means another cation, M, bonded to the silicate sheets present in clay. See chapter 3 for a full discussion of the chemistry of clays.

The concentration of potassium ions in natural waters is less than that of sodium ions because potassium is not as easily

● **Table 2.1** Sample concentrations of ions in sea-water, river-water and rain-water, measured in $mg\,dm^{-3}$

Sea-water	(pH = 8.0)	River-water	(pH = 8.0)	Rain-water	(pH = 5.7)
Cl^-	18 980	HCO_3^-	58.4	Cl^-	3.79
Na^+	10 540	Ca^{2+}	15.0	Na^+	1.98
SO_4^{2-}	2 460	SO_4^{2-}	11.2	SO_4^{2-}	0.58
Mg^{2+}	1 270	Cl^-	7.8	K^+	0.30
Ca^{2+}	400	Na^+	6.3	Mg^{2+}	0.27
K^+	380	Mg^{2+}	4.1	HCO_3^-	0.12
HCO_3^-	140	K^+	2.3	Ca^{2+}	0.09
Br^-	60	Fe^{2+}	0.67		

dissolved out of rocks and is more readily removed from solution by complexing with clays.

The magnesium and calcium ions in river-water come from the weathering of carbonate and silicate rocks, for example:

$$MgCO_3(s) + CO_2(aq) + H_2O(l)$$
$$\longrightarrow Mg^{2+}(aq) + 2HCO_3^-(aq) \quad (2.16)$$

$$MgSiO_3(s) + 2CO_2(aq) + 3H_2O(l)$$
$$\longrightarrow Mg^{2+}(aq) + 2HCO_3^-(aq) + Si(OH)_4(aq) \quad (2.17)$$

Note that silicates can dissolve directly, as described in reaction 2.13, and also dissolve in the presence of carbon dioxide, as described in reaction 2.17. Some of the magnesium ions in sea-water are removed to form magnesium carbonate minerals. The formation of sea shells and corals reduces the concentration in sea-water of both calcium ions and hydrogencarbonate ions, $HCO_3^-(aq)$.

The most abundant anion in sea-water is the chloride ion, $Cl^-(aq)$. Some of this comes from rocks and soils over which the water has passed before reaching the sea. The remainder comes from underwater volcanoes and vents in the seabed. Chlorine exists entirely as chloride ions and does not form stable complexes with any metal ions.

Carbon is present in natural waters as the carbonate ion, $CO_3^{2-}(aq)$, the hydrogencarbonate ion, $HCO_3^-(aq)$, and as dissolved carbon dioxide. The carbon dioxide comes from the air and decay-

ing organic matter. Carbonate ions come from the weathering of carbonate rocks.

The species CO_2, CO_3^{2-} and HCO_3^- are interchangeable depending upon the pH of the water. The equilibria are:

$$CO_2(aq) + H_2O(l) \rightleftharpoons H_2CO_3(aq) \quad (2.18)$$
$$CO_2(aq) + H_2O(l) \rightleftharpoons H^+(aq) + HCO_3^-(aq) \quad (2.19)$$
$$HCO_3^-(aq) \rightleftharpoons H^+(aq) + CO_3^{2-}(aq) \quad (2.20)$$

The species present at particular pH values are shown in figure 2.2.

The pH of natural water depends upon the amounts of dissolved CO_2, HCO_3^-, CO_3^{2-} and OH^-. The equilibria are reactions 2.19 and 2.20 and:

$$HCO_3^-(aq) + H_2O(l) \rightleftharpoons H_2CO_3(aq) + OH^-(aq) \quad (2.21)$$

Solutions containing hydrogencarbonate ions are alkaline due to the predominance of hydroxide ions in reaction 2.21.

In recent hot summers the algae content of some reservoirs has increased. These algae use dissolved carbon dioxide in photosynthesis, causing the equilibrium

$$H_2CO_3(aq) \rightleftharpoons H_2O(l) + CO_2(aq) \quad (2.22)$$

to move to the right. This removes H_2CO_3 and so moves reaction 2.21 to the right, making the water more alkaline.

Dissolved oxygen

Although oxygen is relatively insoluble in water, dissolved oxygen is essential for aquatic life. As with most gases, the dissolving of oxygen in water is an exothermic process and so, at a given pressure, the solubility decreases as the temperature increases (figure 2.3). Solubility is also affected by the turbulence of the water, the concentration of dissolved salts, and the levels of bacterial, plant and animal life.

The lowest concentration of oxygen required for fish to survive is $3\,mg\,dm^{-3}$. Trout and salmon need higher concentrations.

● **Figure 2.2** Species of carbon present at various pH values in natural water.

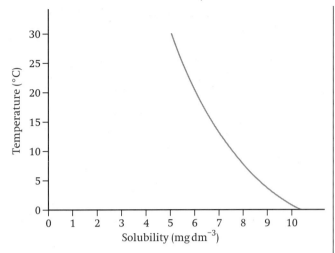

- **Figure 2.3** The variation of the solubility of oxygen in water with temperature.

Organic material rapidly consumes dissolved oxygen with the help of microorganisms:

$$[CH_2O](aq) + O_2(g) \xrightarrow{\text{microorganisms}} CO_2(g) + H_2O(l) \quad (2.23)$$

carbohydrate

Organic materials which reduce the oxygen content of water as they decay are called **oxygen demand chemicals**. They are present in sewage from domestic waste and industrial sources. The food processing industry is particularly responsible for allowing this sort of material to enter the sewage system. Reduced oxygen concentrations affect the water quality and can cause **eutrophication** (see below). The reduced oxygen concentrations, due to the addition of oxygen demand chemicals, means that plants die and decay. Sewage and farm wastes can add to the eutrophication of water.

A way of assessing the oxygen content of water is to measure the **biochemical oxygen demand (BOD)**. This is the amount of oxygen required by bacteria to achieve aerobic oxidation of organic material to carbon dioxide and water. To measure this, an experiment is set up in which a sample of water is saturated with oxygen. It is then allowed to stand at 25 °C for 5 days and the oxygen which remains is measured. The difference between the oxygen levels before and after the 5-day period is the BOD. ('Aerobic' means an environment in which oxygen is present; 'anaerobic' refers to a lack of oxygen.)

Chemical oxygen demand (COD) measures the amount of material in the water that is oxidisable by chemical methods.

There is a natural daily variation in the oxygen levels in water due to daytime photosynthesis and day- and night-time respiration. The level also varies as a consequence of added oxidisable pollutants that decrease the oxygen level. The level is normally restored naturally after a period of time or, in a flowing waterway, further downstream. The time for the oxygen level to restore itself after the addition of a pollutant is called the **recovery time**. Recovery time depends upon the degree of agitation of the water. Greater agitation of the water will result in a larger surface area for air to dissolve in and hence quicker recovery. Thus a fast-flowing river passing over rocks or waterfalls will restore its level of dissolved oxygen much quicker than a still lake or slow river.

What happens at a sewage discharge?

When an organic pollutant enters a river or stream, the concentration of dissolved oxygen decreases due to the oxidation of the organic material by bacteria and protozoa. This is called the **zone of decline** or **decomposition zone**. Animal species such as leeches and snails can survive in this somewhat lower level of oxygen. Following this there is a zone where the level of dissolved oxygen is very low and relatively constant. This is the **damage** or **septic zone**. Here only a few species, such as the sludgeworm and rat-tailed maggot, can survive. The level of oxygen then starts to increase again in the **recovery zone**, where the water starts to clear and sunlight can penetrate. Clean water is then restored. The curve of oxygen concentration produced by these processes is known as a **sag curve** and an example is shown in *figure 2.4*.

SAQ 2.2

Summarise the importance of dissolved oxygen in natural waters. Describe what happens to the level of dissolved oxygen downstream from the introduction of an organic pollutant.

Eutrophication

If too many nutrients enter or are created in a freshwater system, excessive higher plant and algal growth takes place. This makes the water cloudy

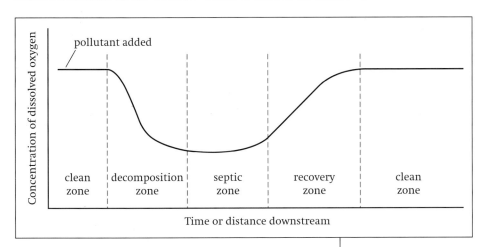

● **Figure 2.4** The variation of dissolved oxygen with time or distance downstream (sag curve).

and unsightly (*figure 2.5*). When these plants and algae die and decay, dissolved oxygen is used up and parts of the water may become anaerobic, causing the formation of foul-smelling substances such as hydrogen sulphide, H_2S, ammonia, NH_3, and thioalcohols, RSH (alcohols in which the functional group contains sulphur instead of oxygen). Some of the nutrients are returned to the water when this happens. This process is called **eutrophication**. Rivers and streams purify themselves quickly, but lakes and static water can become marshy and eventually dry due to an accumulation of incompletely decomposed organic material.

Nitrates and, in particular, phosphates can cause excessive growth of algae. These substances enter

● **Figure 2.5** Algae clogging a ditch at Mildenhall, Suffolk, England. Standing water in this drainage ditch is completely covered with algae fed by nutrients lost from the fields.

freshwater systems from domestic, industrial and agricultural wastes. The use of phosphates in detergents has been a particular source of problems. Eutrophication can be controlled by removal of phosphates from input waters. This is sometimes done by treating input waters with aluminium sulphate in sewage treatment plants; phosphates are precipitated out as aluminium phosphate.

In summer, warm water can float on cold water, because the maximum density of water occurs at temperature 4 °C. This is called **thermal stratification** and it prevents the layers from mixing, so that dissolved oxygen in the top, warm layer does not pass to the cold, bottom layer. If there is a large amount of organic matter in the water, less sunlight will be able to penetrate, thus reducing photosynthesis and the production of oxygen. When the organic matter dies and decays, it falls into the lower layers and soon uses up the dissolved oxygen, creating anaerobic conditions.

SAQ 2.3

Explain the meaning of **eutrophication** in no more than four sentences.

Anionic species in water

The main anionic species in water are phosphate, nitrate, sulphate and carbonate. Their concentrations affect the levels of dissolved oxygen and the growth of aquatic life. Sources of anions are sewage effluent, industrial effluent, farm effluent, run-off from the land, drainage, leaf fall and bird droppings.

Phosphates always occur in the higher oxidation state, +5. In natural water with a pH of 8, the main species are HPO_4^{2-} and $H_2PO_4^{-}$.

Polyphosphates from detergents undergo hydrolysis to give HPO_4^{2-}:

$$P_3O_{10}^{5-}(aq) + 2H_2O(l) \rightleftharpoons 3HPO_4^{2-}(aq) + H^+(aq)$$

(2.24)

The HPO_4^{2-} forms salts which are not very soluble. These end up in sediments or are adsorbed onto clays.

Nitrates are more soluble than phosphates and readily leach from soils into watercourses. The denitrifying bacteria which normally remove nitrates from water are unable to cope with the extra nitrate from the land. The recommended level of nitrate(V), NO_3^-, in drinking water is $10\,mg\,dm^{-3}$. The EU legal limit is $50\,mg\,dm^{-3}$. This is frequently breached in most EU countries.

In very young children, nitrate(V) may be reduced to nitrate(III), nitrite, NO_2^-, by bacteria in the stomach. Young children do not have sufficient acid in their stomachs to prevent the growth of these bacteria. Sometimes this leads to a fatal condition called blue baby syndrome (methaemoglobinaemia) in which nitrate(III) oxidises the iron(II) in haemoglobin to iron(III).

Cyanide from metal cleaning, electroplating and gold extraction sometimes escapes into water systems. It is hydrolysed in water to produce hydrogen cyanide, HCN, which is a weak acid:

$$CN^-(aq) + H_2O(l) \rightleftharpoons HCN(aq) + OH^-(aq) \quad (2.25)$$

As hydrogen cyanide is volatile, the equilibrium in *reaction 2.25* is shifted to the right. Cyanide is highly poisonous as it bonds irreversibly with Fe(III) preventing its reduction to Fe(II) in cells.

The hardness of water

Hard water is a nuisance in many areas. It is difficult to produce a good lather with soap when using hard water. Instead, a white scum is produced which collects in the fibres of clothes and around the edges of sinks and baths. This scum is due to insoluble salts of calcium and magnesium formed by reaction with soap, some of which is therefore removed from solution. Hard water also leads to the 'furring up' of kettles, boilers and pipes. On the other hand, hard water helps create strong teeth and bones, and the incidence of heart disease is lower in hard-water areas.

The hardness is due to dissolved calcium and magnesium ions. These ions find their way into the natural water supply because of the action of dissolved carbon dioxide on carbonate and silicate rocks:

$$\underset{\text{limestone}}{CaCO_3(s)} + H_2O(l) + CO_2(aq) \rightleftharpoons Ca^{2+}(aq) + 2HCO_3^-(aq) \quad (2.26)$$

$$\underset{\text{dolomite}}{CaCO_3.MgCO_3(s)} + 2H_2O(l) + 2CO_2(aq)$$
$$\rightleftharpoons Ca^{2+}(aq) + Mg^{2+}(aq) + 4HCO_3^-(aq) \quad (2.27)$$

$$\underset{\text{silicate}}{MgSiO_3(s)} + 2CO_2(g) + 3H_2O(l)$$
$$\longrightarrow Mg^{2+}(aq) + 2HCO_3^-(aq) + Si(OH)_4(aq) \quad (2.28)$$

Water from limestone and dolomite areas that becomes hard as a result of *reactions 2.26 and 2.27* is said to contain **temporary hardness**. This type of hardness can be removed by boiling the water.

If it is considered necessary to remove the hardness in water, it can be done by one of three methods:

- **Removal of Ca^{2+} and Mg^{2+} as insoluble precipitates**. This can be achieved by boiling the water, thus reversing *reaction 2.26*; because carbon dioxide is removed this reaction can go to completion:

$$Ca^{2+}(aq) + 2HCO_3^-(aq) \longrightarrow CaCO_3(s) + H_2O(l) + CO_2(g) \quad (2.29)$$

  or by adding washing soda, $Na_2CO_3.10H_2O$:

$$Ca^{2+}(aq) + Na_2CO_3(aq) \longrightarrow CaCO_3(s) + 2Na^+(aq) \quad (2.30)$$

  or by adding slaked lime, $Ca(OH)_2$:

$$Ca^{2+}(aq) + HCO_3^-(aq) + OH^-(aq) \longrightarrow CaCO_3(s) + H_2O(l) \quad (2.31)$$

- **The formation of soluble complexes**. Polyphosphates, $P_3O_{10}^{5-}$, are used in detergents to soften water, resulting in the formation of soluble complexes with magnesium and calcium ions:

$$Ca^{2+}(aq) + P_3O_{10}^{5-}(aq) \longrightarrow \underset{\text{soluble}}{CaP_3O_{10}^{3-}(aq)} \quad (2.32)$$

  The detergent molecules themselves can also act as softening agents (R is a long hydrocarbon chain):

$$2ROSO_3^-Na^+(aq) + Ca^{2+}(aq) \longrightarrow \underset{\text{soluble}}{(ROSO_3)_2Ca(aq)} + 2Na^+(aq) \quad (2.33)$$

- **Using ion-exchange resins**. Ion-exchange resins are complex chemical compounds, frequently aluminosilicates, which will exchange either hydrogen or sodium ions for the calcium or magnesium ions in hard water. Hard water is passed through very small beads of resin packed in a cylinder. Ions are exchanged in the cylinder and 'soft' water, without calcium or magnesium ions, comes out of the other end:

$$2resin^-H^+(s) + Ca^{2+}(aq)$$
$$\longrightarrow (resin^-)_2Ca^{2+}(s) + 2H^+(aq) \qquad (2.34)$$

$$2resin^-Na^+(s) + Ca^{2+}(aq)$$
$$\longrightarrow (resin^-)_2Ca^{2+}(s) + 2Na^+(aq) \qquad (2.35)$$

When all the hydrogen or sodium ions on the resin have been exchanged, the resin becomes 'spent'. It can be regenerated by passing concentrated sodium chloride solution through it. The concentration of sodium ions is large enough to replace the calcium ions on the resin:

$$(resin^-)_2Ca^{2+}(s) + 2Na^+(aq)$$
$$\longrightarrow 2resin^-Na^+(s) + Ca^{2+}(aq) \qquad (2.36)$$

When the excess sodium chloride solution has been washed out, the resin is ready for use again.

If sodium aluminium silicate is used as the ion-exchange resin, this is known as the 'Permutit' method of water softening. The method chosen is that which is most appropriate to the situation where water softening is required.

SAQ 2.4

State the ions which cause the hardness in water, explain how limestone produces hardness in water and summarise the use of the process of ion exchange for softening water.

Water supply

A **potable** water supply is one which is drinkable. It must be free of pathogens (disease-causing organisms), have no undesirable tastes, odours, colours or turbidity, and contain no harmful organic or inorganic chemicals. Natural water often has to be treated to make it potable (*figure 2.6*).

It would be difficult, and expensive, to isolate and identify all the possible disease-causing organisms in a water supply. Tests have been devised which estimate the level of bacterial contamination by the 'coliform count', which is a measure

● **Figure 2.6** Water treatment works at Mythe Water Works, Tewkesbury, England.

of the number of *Escherichia coli* bacteria per cubic centimetre. This bacterium rarely causes disease, but its presence in water indicates the likely presence of other disease-causing organisms. As *Escherichia coli* occurs naturally in the intestines of warm-blooded animals, its presence in a water supply suggests faecal pollution. Other coliform bacteria indicate pollution from animal sources, but not necessarily faecal pollution. Directives from the EU and the World Health Organisation require *Escherichia coli* to be absent from public water supplies. It should not be detectable in $100\,cm^3$ of water.

If the water is stored, 50% of the pathogens die within 2 days and 90% within 7 days. Chemical treatment is necessary to remove any that remain. Storage also allows large particles to separate out on standing. This is called **sedimentation**.

Unpleasant taste, odour and colour can be caused by algae in the supply reservoirs. The water is aerated to remove hydrogen sulphide, H_2S, carbon dioxide, CO_2, methane, CH_4, and any other volatile material. Aeration also removes odorous bacteria and oxidises any iron(II) and manganese(II) present. If hardness is considered to be a problem, calcium and magnesium ions are removed in the form of their insoluble carbonates by the addition of washing soda and slaked lime (lime–soda). The high pH of this process also precipitates iron(III) as iron(III) hydroxide, $Fe(OH)_3$, and any manganese ions as manganese(IV) oxide, MnO_2.

Natural waters frequently contain particles which, though solid, are supported by the liquid such that there is very little tendency for the particles to separate out. These particles are called **colloids** and are too small to be visible with an ordinary microscope Their size is generally in the range 1×10^{-9} to 1×10^{-7} m (1 to 100 nm). Colloids and other fine materials are precipitated by adding aluminium sulphate. The aluminium ions hydrolyse to give a gelatinous (jelly-like) hydroxide precipitate, which absorbs other ions and solids as it settles. The charge on the surface of the colloidal particles is neutralised, causing them to coagulate. The high charge density of the aluminium ion, Al^{3+}, neutralises the negative charges on the surface of clay particles, breaking up the layer structure to form a feathery precipitate known as a 'floc'. When this precipitate settles out the process is called **flocculation**.

This use of aluminium ions is being reviewed in Britain following an accident at Camelford, Cornwall, in 1990, when aluminium sulphate was accidentally tipped into the wrong tank at a water treatment plant, resulting in high levels of aluminium in the local water supply. There has been concern since then about the effect of aluminium on health and efforts are being made to reduce the amounts of aluminium used.

Aluminium is toxic to all forms of life: plant, fish, animal and human. In humans, there is a strong link between aluminium and Alzheimer's disease, which results in a loss of memory and mental faculties, particularly in the elderly. The maximum admissible concentration of aluminium in drinking water, as specified in the EU drinking water directive, is $200 \, \mu g \, dm^{-3}$.

Harmful bacteria are killed by the addition of chlorine. Chlorine reacts with water to form chloric(I) acid, HClO (hypochlorous acid):

$$Cl_2(aq) + H_2O(l) \rightleftharpoons H^+(aq) + Cl^-(aq) + HClO(aq) \tag{2.37}$$

In this reaction the chlorine is both oxidised from 0 in chlorine to the +1 state in chloric(I) acid, and reduced to the −1 state in the chloride ion. This simultaneous oxidation and reduction of the same species is called **disproportionation**.

The chloric(I) acid dissociates to give the chlorate(I) (hypochlorite) ion:

$$HClO(aq) \rightleftharpoons H^+(aq) + ClO^-(aq) \tag{2.38}$$

Chloric(I) acid and chlorate(I) ions kill bacteria by oxidation. Chlorate(I) is sometimes added directly to water as sodium chlorate(I) or calcium chlorate(I).

It is important that the oxidising effect of the chloric(I) acid and chlorate(I) ions be maintained during the distribution stage of water supply as well as at the water treatment and storage plant. This is achieved by the addition of ammonia, which produces chloramines:

$$NH_3(aq) + HClO(aq) \longrightarrow NH_2Cl(aq) + H_2O(l) \tag{2.39}$$

$$NH_2Cl(aq) + HClO(aq) \longrightarrow NHCl_2(aq) + H_2O(l) \tag{2.40}$$

$$NHCl_2(aq) + HClO(aq) \longrightarrow NCl_3(aq) + H_2O(l) \tag{2.41}$$

The reaction of the chloramines with water in the distribution system gradually releases chlorate(I) ions, which kill bacteria.

A problem with water chlorination is the production of chlorinated organic matter, such as trichloroalkanes (haloforms), from the low concentration organic pollutants which remain in water. As an alternative, ozone is now being increasingly used to disinfect water.

Organic chemicals, such as pesticides and trichloroalkanes (see above), are removed by passing the water through a filter of granular activated carbon. The EU has set very strict limits on the pesticide content of drinking water. The limit is 1 part of pesticide in 10 000 million parts of water (0.1 ppbv). That is the equivalent of one drop of pesticide in a full-sized swimming pool!

In some countries where eutrophication is a problem, there is an additional process which chemically removes phosphate(V) ions, PO_4^{3-}, by precipitation using aluminium ions, iron(III) ions and the addition of lime. If removal of nitrate(V) is necessary, it is achieved by specialised populations of bacteria working in anaerobic conditions, which convert nitrate to nitrogen gas and water.

Figure 2.7 summarises the various stages in the treatment of raw water to produce potable water.

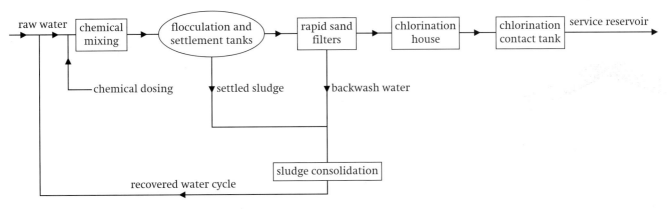

● **Figure 2.7** Layout of typical water treatment plant for public supply.

SUMMARY

◆ Water temperature and gas pressure affect the solubility of gases in water.

◆ Rain-water has a natural acidity due to dissolved carbon dioxide.

◆ The acidity of rain-water is enhanced by dissolved oxides of nitrogen and sulphur.

◆ Dissolved oxygen is important in the support of aquatic life and in the decomposition of organic material.

◆ Temporary hardness of water is caused by dissolved calcium and magnesium ions, which can be removed by boiling and ion exchange.

◆ To obtain water that is drinkable, natural water undergoes a series of physical, chemical and biological processes.

◆ Bacteria are removed from water supplies by oxidation using chlorine or ozone.

Questions

1 **a** Identify an ion which, when present in water, causes the water to be hard.

b Explain why its presence prevents the ready formation of a lather with soap.

c Explain how limestone can produce hardness in water.

d Describe the removal of temporary hardness from water by boiling and ion exchange. Explain the chemistry involved.

2 Describe and explain the preparation of potable water by the separation of solid material, precipitation by using aluminium ions, $Al^{3+}(aq)$, and purification.

CHAPTER 3

The lithosphere

By the end of this chapter you should be able to:

1 explain the chemical processes of weathering;

2 describe the structure of clay minerals;

3 explain the process of cation exchange at the surface of clays;

4 explain the availability of plant nutrients in terms of the pH and oxygen content of the soil.

Most of the **lithosphere** is composed of rocks and clays which are made of silicates and aluminosilicates. Because the bond energy of the Si–O bond is high at $468\,kJ\,mol^{-1}$, silicates are resistant to chemical attack. Silicates therefore resist weathering and persist in the environment. In aluminosilicates some silicon atoms are replaced by aluminium. These aluminosilicates are the basis of feldspars and clays.

Types of rock

The rocks of the Earth are of three kinds: igneous, sedimentary and metamorphic.

● **Figure 3.1** Fingal's Cave on the island of Staffa off the west coast of Scotland, showing columnar basalt.

Igneous rocks

Igneous rocks are made from the cooled liquid magma from beneath the Earth's crust. They are of two types: intrusive and extrusive.

Intrusive igneous rocks are formed from magma that has cooled slowly beneath the surface of the Earth. Because of the slow cooling these rocks consist of large crystals. Granite is the most common intrusive igneous rock. It has large crystalline grains of mica, quartz and feldspar, and contains 73% silicon dioxide by mass. As it is formed at great depths, granite is only exposed where ancient earth movements have lifted the rocks. Thus granite is found in the highlands of Britain, for example in the Scottish Highlands and the Dartmoor tors.

Extrusive igneous rocks have cooled rapidly on the Earth's surface, often from magma emitted from volcanoes, and they therefore consist of small crystals. Basalt is a common extrusive igneous rock and contains on average 52% silicon dioxide by mass. Often it weathers into hexagonal columns, as at the Giant's Causeway in Northern Ireland and Fingal's Cave on the Isle of Staffa off the west coast of Scotland (*figure 3.1*).

Sedimentary rocks

The formation of sedimentary rocks starts with the weathering of other rocks by sun, wind, rain, frost and chemical processes. The broken-up material is transported, mainly by water, and deposited in rivers, lakes and the sea in the form of loose sediments.

The loose sediments settle out onto the river bed or the seabed and are cemented together with minerals such as silica, SiO_2, calcite, $CaCO_3$, dolomite, $CaCO_3.MgCO_3$, gypsum, $CaSO_4.2H_2O$, anhydrite, $CaSO_4$, and iron oxides. They are compressed by the weight of overlying material into various kinds of sedimentary rock.

■ Oolitic limestone (*figure 3.2*) contains very small chalky spheres cemented together. It has a creamy colour and is used as a building stone.

● **Figure 3.2** Oolitic limestone with fossils.

■ Chalk (*figure 3.3*) is a pure form of limestone. It is brilliant white when freshly exposed, fine grained, and permeable. It often contains flints and fossils.

● **Figure 3.3** Chalk.

■ Sandstone (*figure 3.4*) is composed of small, rounded quartz granules which appear glassy.

● **Figure 3.4** Sandstone.

These granules are cemented together with feldspar minerals. The red and brown sand-stones derive their colour from iron oxides.

■ Conglomerates are composed of rounded pebbles from many different types of rock cemented together by silica or calcite.

Sandstone and conglomerate are examples of clastic sedimentary rocks, that is they are formed from fragments of rocks.

Metamorphic rocks

When rocks are heated and/or compressed inside the Earth they recrystallise while still remaining solid. Crystalline metamorphic rocks result (*figure 3.5*). New minerals frequently form in this process.

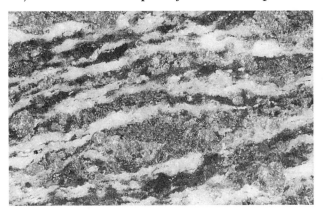

● **Figure 3.5** Metamorphic rock, showing the layer structure.

The compression results in minerals being lined up in the same direction: such rocks are said to be **foliated**. Examples are slate, schist and gneiss.

■ Slate splits into thin sheets along planes (called cleavage planes).

■ Schist is a medium- to coarse-grained rock in which mica grains can easily be seen lined up

Name	Original rock	Cause of formation	Minerals contained	Grain size
marble	limestone	heat	calcite	medium
metaquartzite	sandstone	heat	quartz	medium
schist	mudstone	heat and pressure	mica, quartz, feldspar, garnet	medium to coarse
gneiss	mudstone	heat and pressure	mica, quartz, feldspar, hornblende	medium to coarse
slate	mudstone	pressure	mica, quartz, feldspar	very fine
hornfels	mudstone	heat	quartz, feldspar, pyroxene	fine to medium

● **Table 3.1** Metamorphic rocks.

in the same plane. Quartz and feldspar are the other minerals present in schist.

■ Gneiss is coarse grained with obvious banding.

■ Hornfels is a metamorphic rock formed by heat alone. The rock is unfoliated and the minerals are not lined up.

Some metamorphic rocks are described in *table 3.1*.

During metamorphism, new mineral groupings are produced which depend on the pressure and temperature when the new rocks were formed. Important metamorphic minerals are muscovite mica, $KAl_2AlSi_3O_{10}(OH)_2$, biotite mica, $K(Mg,Fe)_5(Al,Fe^{3+})_2Si_3O_{10}(OH)_8$, pyroxenes, for example $NaAlSi_2O_6$, and the garnets, for example $Ca_3Cr_2(SiO_4)_3$.

Chemical weathering of rocks

Weathering is the breaking-down of rocks and rock surfaces by the action of water, oxygen and carbon dioxide. The chemical processes of weathering are dissolving, hydration, carbonation, hydrolysis, oxidation and reduction.

Dissolving and hydration

The most common soluble ionic materials in the Earth's crust are sodium chloride (solubility $350\,g\,dm^{-3}$) and calcium sulphate (gypsum and anhydrite, $2\,g\,dm^{-3}$). Silica is slightly soluble ($6.5 \times 10^{-3}\,g\,dm^{-3}$):

$$SiO_2(s) + 2H_2O(l) \rightleftharpoons H_4SiO_4(aq)$$
silicic acid
(3.1)

The solubility of ionic solids can be explained in terms of their lattice enthalpy and the enthalpy change of hydration of their ions.

■ The lattice is broken up into free 'gaseous' ions. The energy necessary to do this is equal to the reverse of the **lattice enthalpy** (−LE). The lattice enthalpy is the energy given out when 1 mole of a crystalline lattice is formed from its constituent ions in the gaseous state under standard conditions.

■ The individual ions are then hydrated with a sheath of water molecules. The energy change for this process is the enthalpy change of hydration. *Table 3.2* shows that smaller ions have a greater attraction for water molecules. (The hydration number is the average number of water molecules held within the influence of a particular ion.) As the size of the ion increases, the same charge is

same charge spread over larger surface area, therefore less charge density

● **Figure 3.6** Charge density on an ion.

Ion	Ionic radius (nm)	Charge density charge/radius	Hydration number	$\Delta H_{hydration}$ (kJ mol^{-1})
Li$^+$	0.060	16.7	25.3	−498
Na$^+$	0.095	10.5	16.6	−393
K$^+$	0.133	7.5	10.5	−310
Rb$^+$	0.148	6.8	10.0	−284
Cs$^+$	0.169	5.9	9.9	−251

● **Table 3.2** Ions of Group I elements.

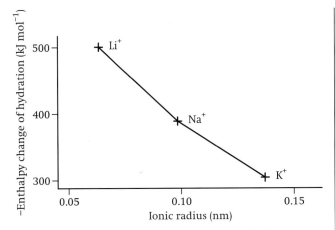

● **Figure 3.7** Effect of ionic radius on hydration.

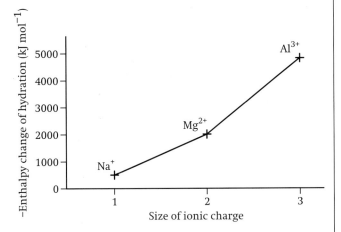

● **Figure 3.8** Effect of ionic charge on hydration.

spread over a larger surface area, therefore the charge density is lower (*figure 3.6*) and the enthalpy change of hydration is lower (*figure 3.7*).

Similarly, if the ion size remains constant and the number of charges increases, the charge density will also increase leading to an increase in the enthalpy change of hydration (*figure 3.8*).

So the enthalpy change of solution is given by:

$$\Delta H_{solution} = - LE + \Delta H_{hydration}$$

The process may be represented by an energy cycle (*figure 3.9*).

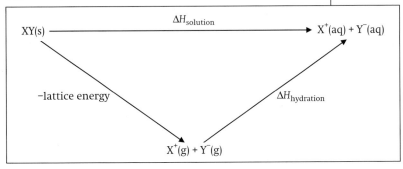

● **Figure 3.9** The energy cycle for the dissolving of an ionic solid.

The enthalpy change of solution, $\Delta H_{solution}$, is quite often small in value compared with the values of lattice enthalpy and enthalpy change of hydration. For a positive value of $\Delta H_{solution}$ the substance becomes more soluble as the temperature rises. For a negative value the opposite applies.

The most soluble ions have a low charge and a large radius, for example caesium, rubidium and potassium.

Ions with a high charge and a small radius may hydrolyse in water to give insoluble hydroxides. For example:

$$Al^{3+}(aq) + 3H_2O(l) \rightleftharpoons Al(OH)_3(s) + 3H^+(aq) \qquad (3.2)$$

The high charge density of the aluminium ion weakens one of the O–H bonds. Clay minerals thus eventually weather to form bauxite, Al_2O_3. Minerals containing iron(III) similarly weather to give haematite, Fe_2O_3.

The solubility of many minerals is dependent on pH. For example, the solubility of silicon dioxide is increased by a higher pH because the following equilibrium moves to the right:

$$H_4SiO_4(aq) \rightleftharpoons H^+(aq) + H_3SiO_4^-(aq) \qquad (3.3)$$

This then pulls *reaction 3.1* to the right also and more silicon dioxide dissolves.

Carbonation

The reaction of carbon dioxide dissolved in water with materials in the Earth's crust is referred to as **carbonation**. Carbon dioxide reacts with water to form an acidic solution (see chapter 2, page 29):

$$CO_2(g) + H_2O(l) \rightleftharpoons H^+(aq) + HCO_3^-(aq) \qquad (3.4)$$

The acidic solution reacts further with minerals such as calcium carbonate:

$$CaCO_3(s) + H^+(aq) \\ \rightleftharpoons Ca^{2+}(aq) + HCO_3^-(aq) \qquad (3.5)$$

The overall reaction may be written as:

$$CaCO_3(s) + CO_2(g) + H_2O(l) \\ \rightleftharpoons Ca^{2+}(aq) + 2HCO_3^-(aq) \qquad (3.6)$$

This reaction causes rapid weathering of calcium carbonate minerals. Limestone caves and the grykes

● **Figure 3.10** Limestone pavement showing clints and grykes in the Yorkshire Dales, England.

found on limestone pavements are an example of this reaction (*figure 3.10*). Sometimes so much limestone dissolves and collapses that a deep vertical sink hole or swallow hole is formed. A well-known example is Gaping Ghyll near Ingleborough in the Yorkshire Dales, England, which is 120 metres deep.

When water drips from a cave roof, carbon dioxide is lost to the air, the reverse of *reaction 3.6*

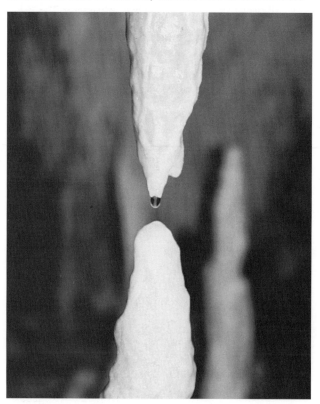

● **Figure 3.11** Stalactites and stalagmites. This stalactite (growing down) has almost met the stalagmite (growing up), which has been formed from the same drops of water.

takes place and minute amounts of solid calcium carbonate form. These build up to form stalactites hanging from the roof. A similar process takes place when the water drop hits the floor, causing stalagmites to grow upwards from the floor (*figure 3.11*).

When water rich in dissolved calcium carbonate is aerated, for example at waterfalls, carbon dioxide is again lost and calcium carbonate is deposited as tufa.

Limestone areas which have their landforms produced mainly by carbonation are said to have karst landscapes, as in the Yorkshire Dales, England.

Hydrolysis

Hydrolysis is the reaction of water with some other species, leading to the breaking of an O–H bond and the formation of an acidic or alkaline solution.

■ An example of the formation of an acidic solution is:

$$SO_2(g) + H_2O(l) \rightleftharpoons 2H^+(aq) + SO_3^{2-}(aq) \qquad (3.7)$$

■ An example of the formation of an alkaline solution is:

$$CaO(s) + H_2O(l) \rightleftharpoons Ca(OH)_2(aq) \qquad (3.8)$$

Hydrolytic weathering of minerals occurs by the breaking of an O–H bond and also possibly an M–O bond (M is a metal atom). The metals with the weakest M–O bonds weather first and are most easily removed from the rock (*table 3.3*).

The eventual end-point of all chemical weathering is the formation of insoluble oxides, for example silicon dioxide, SiO_2, aluminium oxide, Al_2O_3, and iron(III) oxide, Fe_2O_3.

Bond	Strength (kJ mol^{-1})
Mg–O	377
Mn–O	389
Fe–O	389
Ca–O	423
Si–O	464
Al–O	582
Ti–O	674

● **Table 3.3** Strength of M–O bonds.

Oxidation and reduction

Oxidation and reduction are important processes in the weathering of rocks. These processes can occur where cations and anions have more than one oxidation state, for example iron(II) and iron(III), manganese(II) and manganese(IV), copper(I) and copper(II), and sulphur(−II), sulphur(IV) and sulphur(VI). Remember that oxidation is the removal of electrons from a species and reduction is the addition of electrons.

Both iron and sulphur are oxidised when iron pyrites, FeS_2, is weathered:

$$2FeS_2(s) + 7O_2 + 2H_2O \longrightarrow 2Fe^{2+}(aq) + 4SO_4^{2-}(aq) + 4H^+(aq) \qquad (3.9)$$

$$2Fe^{2+}(aq) + \tfrac{1}{2}O_2(g) + 2H^+(aq) \longrightarrow 2Fe^{3+}(aq) + H_2O(l) \qquad (3.10)$$

$$2Fe^{3+}(aq) + 6H_2O(l) \longrightarrow 2Fe(OH)_3(s) + 6H^+(aq) \qquad (3.11)$$

SAQ 3.1

Describe the changes in oxidation number for iron and sulphur in *reactions 3.9–3.11*.

SAQ 3.2

Give oxidation number changes for the following weathering processes:

a $MnSiO_3(s) + \tfrac{1}{2}O_2(g) + 2H_2O(l) \longrightarrow MnO_2(s) + H_4SiO_4(aq)$
rhodonite

b $MnCO_3(s) + \tfrac{1}{2}O_2(g) + H_2O(l) \longrightarrow MnO_2(s) + H_2CO_3(aq)$
rhodochrosite

c $PbS(s) + 2O_2(g) \longrightarrow PbSO_4(s)$
galena

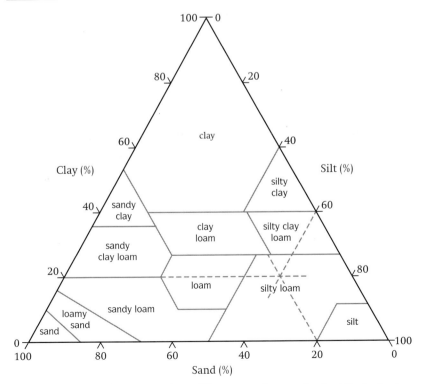

● **Figure 3.12** Soil texture chart. The example, marked with dashed lines, consists of 60% silt, 20% sand and 20% clay; it is a silty loam.

Soil

From a chemist's viewpoint, soil is a mixture of inorganic and organic materials with particle sizes ranging from colloidal (see chapter 2, page 36) to small stones. It contains water and gases in variable proportions, and, of course, some living material. Soil texture is determined by the relative proportions of these constituents in the soil (*figure 3.12*).

The principal inorganic constituents of soil are sand, silt and clay in varying proportions.

■ Sand is mainly quartz, SiO_2, of particle size 0.05–2.0 mm (fine sand is 0.05–0.1 mm; coarse sand is 1.0–2.0 mm). Sandy soils are light and easy to dig, but because of the relatively large particle size they allow water to pass through easily. Thus soluble mineral salts are easily leached from sandy soils.

■ Silt is again mainly quartz plus other silicates, but with particles of a much smaller size (0.002–0.05 mm).

■ Clay particles have diameters less than 0.002 mm and consist of silicate and aluminosilicate minerals.

The movement of water and gases through the soil is related to the number and size of spaces between the particles. This is determined in part by the average particle size, which depends upon the proportions of sand, silt and clay in the soil.

Clay has the smallest particles, therefore the number of spaces between the particles is greatest in a given volume. These spaces are small enough to produce capillary action, which drags water into the clay. Clay therefore has a greater water-holding capacity than sandy soil, but much of this water is bound to minerals or is contained in microscopic pores and is therefore unavailable to plants. Sandy soils have a low water-holding capacity, but most of the water is available to plants.

The water in soil contains dissolved minerals that act as nutrients for plants. The amount and composition of the dissolved nutrients depends on the pH of the soil solution, so both acidic and basic pollutants can affect the nutrient composition of soil water.

The air in soil has a similar composition to that in the troposphere, but it is richer in carbon dioxide because of decay processes.

Normally the physical and chemical conditions favour oxidation, which helps in the decay of organic material. However, in a waterlogged soil reduction can occur, leading to a change in the products of the decomposition of organic matter. In reducing conditions, anaerobic bacteria predominate and the products of decomposition are volatile carboxylic acids and ethene instead of carbon dioxide.

Clay minerals

Clays consist of silicate and aluminosilicate minerals. They have a layered structure. There are three basic types of clay known as 1:1, 2:1 and 2:2. These ratios refer to the arrangement of the two different sheet structures in the clay.

One type of sheet consists of SiO_4^{4-} tetrahedra with three corners shared (*figure 3.13*). The oxygen atoms at the fourth corners of the tetrahedra (all these corners point in the same direction) are also involved with the second sheet. Some of the silicon atoms in this sheet may be substituted by aluminium in varying amounts.

SAQ 3.3

Draw a dot and cross diagram of the silicate ion.

The second type of sheet is made up of close-packed oxygen atoms and hydroxyl groups arranged as octahedra, with aluminium, or some-

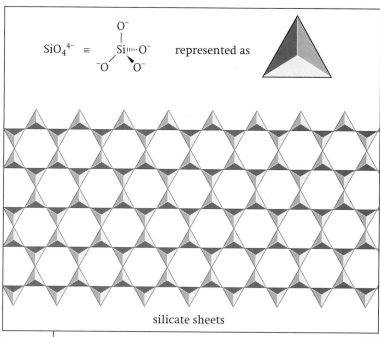

silicate sheets

● **Figure 3.13** Silicate ions are able to form a silicate sheet by sharing three corners with other silicate ions.

times magnesium, in the octahedral holes – the metal atom is surrounded by six oxygen atoms, for example a basic unit of AlO_6 (*figure 3.14*).

Clays contain both types of sheets mostly in the ratio one tetrahedral sheet to one octahedral sheet, known as a 1:1 clay, or two tetrahedral sheets to one octahedral sheet, known as a 2:1 clay.

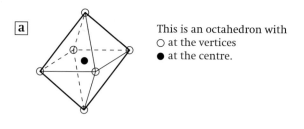

a This is an octahedron with ○ at the vertices ● at the centre.

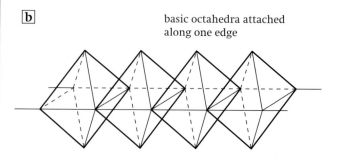

b basic octahedra attached along one edge

● **Figure 3.14 a** The basic octahedral AlO_6 unit. **b** Part of an octahedral sheet.

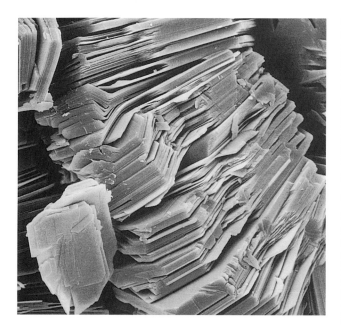

● **Figure 3.15** Photomicrograph of kaolinite showing the layer structure.

Kaolinite is a 1:1 clay (*figure 3.15*). There is one tetrahedral sheet and one octahedral sheet in each layer, the layers being held together by hydrogen bonding between oxygen atoms of the tetrahedral sheets and hydroxyl groups of the octahedral sheets (*figure 3.16*). Because of the hydrogen bonding, water cannot enter between the layers, so kaolinite does not expand on wetting. The relatively weak nature of hydrogen bonding means kaolinite can be easily broken up between the fingers. These properties make kaolinite suitable for use as modelling clay.

Examples of 2:1 clays are vermiculite and mont-morillonite. In this arrangement there is little attraction between the silicate oxygens of the tetrahedral sheets in different layers (*figure 3.17*), thus water and cations can enter the space between the layers. This water can force the layers

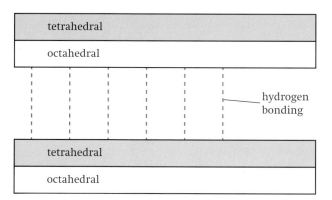

● **Figure 3.16** 1:1 clay.

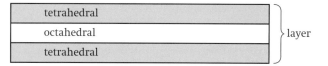

● **Figure 3.17** 2:1 clay.

apart, exposing a large internal surface area and causing the clay to expand when wet. This makes soils containing 2:1 clays difficult to plough and dig. When these soils dry, the opposite effect takes place and the soil shrinks and cracks (*figure 3.18*).

In 2:1 clays such as montmorillonite and vermiculite, some aluminium ions, Al^{3+}, in the octahedral sheet are substituted by magnesium ions, Mg^{2+}. This leaves individual layers with a high negative charge. Vermiculite also has one quarter of the silicon(IV) atoms replaced by aluminium ions, so the negative charge is greater still.

The large surface area of these clays with a high negative charge attracts cations that are hydrated (*figure 3.19*). This gives the wet clay its sticky feel. These cations can also be exchanged with other cations contained in the surrounding soil solution. This property of 2:1 clays, known as the permanent cation-exchange capacity, is an important feature in the retention and supply of cationic nutrients to plants (see page 47).

● **Figure 3.18** Dried out, cracked 2:1 clay.

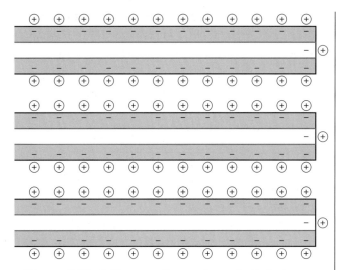

● **Figure 3.19** Cations on the surface of a 2:1 clay.

A 2:2 clay is similar to a 2:1 clay, but it contains an extra second sheet in which some of the aluminium atoms are replaced by magnesium and iron atoms. An example of a 2:2 clay is chlorite.

Table 3.4 is a comparison of 1:1 and 2:1 clays.

SAQ 3.4

Explain why the addition of aluminium ions causes clay particles to flocculate. (As we saw on page 36 a 'floc' is a feathery precipitate. When such a precipitate settles out the process is called **flocculation**.)

Organic matter

Organic matter in soil can be divided into non-humic and humic types.

■ Non-humic material is the undecomposed or partly decomposed fragments of plants and soil organisms.

■ Humic material is called **humus**, and is a complex mixture of brown amorphous and colloidal substances modified from the original plant and animal tissue by microorganisms. The compounds it contains are highly polymerised. As humus forms, the cellulose material is broken down but the protein is retained. Humus influences the water-holding capacity of a soil, its ion-exchange capacity and the binding of metal ions. Lone pairs of electrons on the nitrogen atoms of long protein molecules are able to donate into empty orbitals on metal ions, forming a ring structure called a **chelate**:

In this way essential metal micronutrients are held in the soil by the humus and are prevented

Similarities	
Layer silicates	
Contain tetrahedral 'SiO$_4$' sheets joined to octahedral 'AlO$_6$' sheets	
Outer surface of clay particles attract hydrated cations	
Water hydrogen bonded to oxide ions on surface of silicate tetrahedra; this water not available to plants	
Differences	
1:1	**1:2**
Hydrogen bonding between layers	Very little attraction between silicate oxygens of tetrahedral sheets in different layers
	Water and cations can enter space between layers
Does not expand when wet	Expands when wet because can absorb more water
Easily broken up	
Easy to plough	Difficult to plough and dig
Used as modelling clay	Sticky when wet
	Shrinks and cracks when dry
One SiO$_4$ sheet to one AlO$_6$ sheet	Two SiO$_4$ sheets to one AlO$_6$ sheet
Relatively small surface area per unit mass	Relatively large surface area per unit mass due to large internal surface area between layers
Can exchange cations from outer surface only	Can exchange cations from outer and inner surfaces
Relatively low negative charge on surface	High negative charge on surface
Low cation-exchange capacity	High cation-exchange capacity

● **Table 3.4** A comparison of 1:1 and 2:1 clay minerals.

from being leached out. They are slowly released in the process of ion exchange and are taken up by plants through their roots.

The properties of soil

Ion-exchange capacity and soil pH are inter-related and influence the availability of plant nutrients. Pollutants can affect both of these properties.

Ion-exchange capacity

The ion-exchange capacity of a soil means its ability to hold and exchange ions. Clays have a large surface area and are therefore good ion exchangers. As explained earlier, clays containing aluminium are permanently anionic and are able to hold hydrated cations, M^+, at their surface:

$$clay^-(s) + M^+(aq) \longrightarrow clay-M(s) \qquad (3.12)$$

These cations can be replaced by different ions from the soil solution in a process called cation exchange:

$$clay-M(s) + M'^+(aq) \rightleftharpoons clay-M'(s) + M^+(aq) \qquad (3.13)$$

These cation-exchange properties are permanent as a result of ion exchange within the mineral.

The cation-exchange capacity of a clay mineral is measured as the number of moles of exchangeable positive charge held by 1 kg of the mineral. Examples are $1.5 \, mol \, kg^{-1}$ for vermiculite, $1.0 \, mol \, kg^{-1}$ for montmorillonite and $0.3 \, mol \, kg^{-1}$ for kaolinite.

The surface of a clay consists of layers of oxides and hydroxides. Exchange at the surface is affected by pH. At high pH the hydroxyl group loses protons, or the protons are replaced by metal ions:

$$clay-OH(s) \rightleftharpoons clay-O^-(s) + H^+(aq) \qquad (3.14)$$

$$clay-OH(s) + M^+(aq) \rightleftharpoons clay-OM(s) + H^+(aq) \qquad (3.15)$$

Similarly, organic acids in soils can act as cation exchangers:

$$R-C\!\!\begin{array}{c}O\\\\OH\end{array}(s) + M^+(aq) \rightleftharpoons R-C\!\!\begin{array}{c}O\\\\OM\end{array}(s) + H^+(aq) \qquad (3.16)$$

These ion-exchange processes are important in plant nutrition (*figure 3.20*). For example, if potassium ions are taken out of solution by plants, clays release potassium ions from clay–K back into the solution to re-establish equilibrium – the clay acts as a reservoir of nutrient cations:

$$clay-K(s) + H_2O(l) \rightleftharpoons clay-H(s) + K^+(aq) + OH^-(aq) \qquad (3.17)$$

Some herbicides, such as paraquat and simazine, may affect this process, because they are adsorbed onto the surface charges of soil particles, even though they are said to become 'inactive' in the soil.

● **Figure 3.20** A vine leaf grown **a** with and **b** without the nutrient potassium.

Clays also have an anion-exchange capacity:

clay–OH(s) + A⁻(aq)
$$\rightleftharpoons \text{clay–A(s)} + \text{OH}^-\text{(aq)} \quad (3.18)$$

Nitrate ions are only held weakly, and are easily washed out, so clay soils are not good retainers of the nitrate nutrient, NO_3^-. Phosphate, PO_4^{3-}, is strongly held, especially in clays with a high aluminium and iron content. This means that much of the phosphate added to clay soil becomes bonded to the clay and is not available to plants. [As a class experiment you may wish to investigate the ion-exchange properties of some soils.]

SAQ 3.5

Explain how cation exchange on the surface of clays can maintain a constant supply of cationic nutrients to plants when needed.

Soil pH

The pH of a solution is a measure of its acidity or alkalinity. It is defined as the negative logarithm of the hydrogen ion concentration:

$$pH = -\log_{10}[H^+(aq)]$$

Soil pH is a very important factor in plant growth and the normal range is from 3 to 9. Large amounts of humus in the soil induce acidity, since humus contains a high proportion of carboxylic acid, $-CO_2H$, groups. This may be counterbalanced if high concentrations of basic cations are present. A pH close to 7 in soils is associated with large amounts of exchangeable calcium.

Acidity can also be induced by the presence of significant quantities of aluminium in solution. This generally comes from the weathering of rocks and clays. A lower pH encourages this weathering process:

$$\text{Al}_2\text{Si}_2\text{O}_5\text{(OH)}_4\text{(s)} + 6\text{H}^+\text{(aq)} \longrightarrow 2\text{Al}^{3+}\text{(aq)} + 2[\text{Si(OH)}_4]\text{(s)} + \text{H}_2\text{O(l)}$$
$$\text{kaolinite} \quad (3.19)$$

As the aluminium ion has a high charge density, it complexes with water and then regenerates hydrogen ions:

$$[\text{Al(H}_2\text{O)}_6]^{3+}\text{(aq)} \longrightarrow [\text{Al(OH)(H}_2\text{O)}_5]^{2+}\text{(aq)} + \text{H}^+\text{(aq)}$$
$$\longrightarrow [\text{Al(OH)}_2\text{(H}_2\text{O)}_4]^+\text{(aq)} + 2\text{H}^+\text{(aq)} \quad (3.20)$$

Aluminium ions adhere strongly to exchange sites on clays because of their high charge, and they maintain the local acidity as a result of *reaction 3.20*. A similar situation applies to the hydrated iron(III) ion, $[\text{Fe(H}_2\text{O)}_6]^{3+}$, which is also released as a result of the weathering of clays.

Cations adsorbed onto the surface of clays affect the pH when they are released. For example, the pH is raised by:

$$\text{clay–Na(s)} + \text{H}_2\text{O(l)} \rightleftharpoons \text{clay–H(s)} + \text{Na}^+\text{(aq)} + \text{OH}^-\text{(aq)} \quad (3.21)$$

and is lowered by:

$$\text{clay–Al(s)} + 4\text{H}_2\text{O(l)} \rightleftharpoons \text{clay–H}_3\text{(s)} + \text{Al(OH)}_4^-\text{(aq)} + \text{H}^+\text{(aq)} \quad (3.22)$$

Availability of plant nutrients

If a soil has a high proportion of its cation-exchange sites occupied by hydrogen ions, it will not be able to supply plants with the nutrients they need.

SAQ 3.6

Explain how and why the pH of the soil influences the surface cation-exchange capacity of clay minerals.

In an acidic medium, nitrate(V) ions, NO_3^-, may be reduced to ammonium ions, NH_4^+:

$$\text{NO}_3^-\text{(aq)} + 10\text{H}^+\text{(aq)} + 8e^- \longrightarrow \text{NH}_4^+\text{(aq)} + 3\text{H}_2\text{O(l)} \quad (3.23)$$

Plants are usually only able to accept nutrients in an oxidised form, hence increased acidity of the soil reduces the availability of nitrogen for plant growth. To maintain nitrogen in an oxidised form, a well-aerated soil is necessary to provide a sufficient supply of oxygen to enable the reverse of *reaction 3.23* to take place.

The effect of soil pH on the availability of nutrients is shown in *table 3.5*.

Points to note from *table 3.5*:
- Calcium and magnesium are removed from soil solution at high pH because they form insoluble carbonates.
- Little iron, manganese or aluminium is found in solution above pH6 because of the formation of insoluble hydroxides.

Nutrients	pH								
	3	4	5	6	7	8	9	10	11
calcium magnesium	maximum availability						form insoluble carbonates		
iron manganese aluminium	maximum availability				form insoluble hydroxides				
phosphorus	forms insoluble iron and aluminium phosphates				maximum availability		forms insoluble calcium phosphate		
nitrogen sulphur	nitrate reduced to ammonium				maximum availability				
potassium	reduced availability				maximum availability				
copper zinc	reduced availability				maximum availability		form insoluble hydroxides		

● **Table 3.5** Effect of soil pH on the availability of nutrients.

■ Iron may be present in soil as iron(II) ions, particularly in marshy areas. This has two disadvantages: (i) plants can usually only accept nutrients in the oxidised form, as stated earlier, and (ii) the reduced form is more soluble and can be more easily washed out of the soil. Conditions are needed which favour iron(III) ions. A higher pH, up to but not above 6.0, and a good supply of oxygen from a well-aerated soil will increase the rate of oxidation of iron(II) to iron(III) – the same conditions which favour the maintenance of nitrogen as nitrate(V), preventing reduction to ammonium, and which give the maximum availability of phosphate.

■ At a low pH, nitrogen is less available as a nutrient because of the reduction of nitrate(V) to ammonium (*reaction 3.23*).

■ The availability of the nutrient phosphate is greatest at a pH of between 6 and 7. This is because the most soluble form of phosphate is $H_2PO_4^-$, which exists over the range pH2–7. However, below pH6 insoluble iron and aluminium phosphates form, and above pH7 insoluble calcium phosphate forms.

SAQ 3.7

What are the soil conditions which will best ensure a good supply of the plant nutrients iron(III), nitrate(V) and phosphate? Explain in each case why these conditions are appropriate.

To ensure the best conditions for available nutrients the soil pH needs to be carefully controlled. To a certain extent, soil pH is controlled by natural systems. The equilibria present when carbon dioxide dissolves in water were mentioned in chapter 2 (page 29). Hydrogencarbonate ions, HCO_3^-, can remove some of the hydrogen ions, thus acting as a buffer:

$$HCO_3^-(aq) + H^+(aq) \rightleftharpoons H_2CO_3(aq)$$
$$\rightleftharpoons CO_2(g) + H_2O(l) \qquad (3.24)$$

However, you will recall from *figure 2.2* (page 31) that below pH4.5 there are virtually no hydrogencarbonate ions, therefore there is a limit to this buffering action. Humus also has a buffering action as it contains organic acids:

$$RCO_2^-(s) + 2H^+(aq) \rightleftharpoons RCO_2H(s) + H^+(aq)$$
$$\rightleftharpoons RCO_2H_2^+(s) \qquad (3.25)$$

Artificial increases in soil pH are achieved by liming the ground using calcium carbonate (limestone) or calcium hydroxide (*figure 3.21*). This is usually done once every five to ten years as the liming material is only lost relatively slowly from the soil by leaching because of its low solubility. *Table 3.6* gives the lime requirements of various soils.

Liming works as follows:

$$clay-H_2(s) + CaCO_3(s)$$
$$\longrightarrow clay-Ca(s) + H_2O(l) + CO_2(g) \qquad (3.26)$$

$$clay-Ca(s) + 2H_2O(l)$$
$$\rightleftharpoons clay-H_2(s) + Ca^{2+}(aq) + 2OH^-(aq) \qquad (3.27)$$

Initial pH of soil	Loamy sands	Sandy loams	Loams Silty loams Organic sandy loams	Clay loams Organic loams Peat loams	Clays Organic clay loams Peat
6.0	20	25	30	40	50
5.5	40	50	65	80	100
5.0	60	75	95	120	150
4.5	80	95	130	160	190
4.0	100	120	160	200	240
3.5	120	145	190	245	290

● **Table 3.6** Lime requirements of various soils (measured in tonnes per hectare).

● **Figure 3.21** Spreading lime on ploughed hill pasture in Shropshire, England, prior to grass sowing. Liming of soils increases their pH.

Different clay minerals require differing amounts of lime to be added. When lime is added to soil the pH changes very little at first, then slowly rises. This is because the soil acts as a buffer. Hydrogen ions attached to particles of soil replace the hydrogen ions in soil solution when they are removed. The amount of base that needs to be added to bring a soil to the desired pH is known as the soil's **buffering capacity**. *Figure 3.22* shows the buffering capacity of various clay minerals.

Sometimes the efficacy of liming is affected by 'acid surges' following the melting of ice and snow that was formed from acidified water. These surges involve a rapid release of a large quantity of acidic water, which a previous liming may be unable to neutralise.

On rare occasions when it is necessary to lower soil pH, this is done by adding acid salts such as ammonium sulphate:

$$NH_4^+(aq) \rightleftharpoons NH_3(aq) + H^+(aq) \qquad (3.28)$$

$$clay^-(s) + H^+(aq) \rightleftharpoons clay{-}H(s) \qquad (3.29)$$

[You may wish to do experiments on the determination of soil pH and the determination of the lime requirement of a soil.]

SAQ 3.8

Which clay has the lowest buffering capacity? Explain your answer in terms of *figure 3.22* and the structure of the clay.

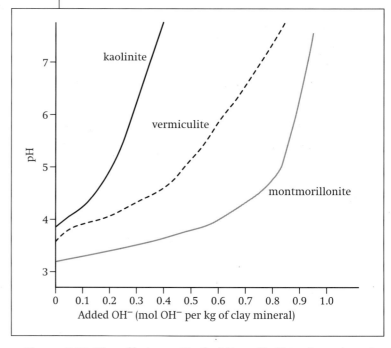

● **Figure 3.22** The effect on pH of adding alkali to clay minerals.

SUMMARY

◆ Chemical weathering of rocks can be explained in terms of the hydration of ions, the precipitation of carbonates and the ultimate formation of insoluble oxides.

◆ Clay minerals are made of layers of 'SiO$_4$' tetrahedra and 'AlO$_6$' octahedra arranged as either 1:1 or 2:1 structures.

◆ Cation exchange can take place at the surface of silicate clays. This is important in the supply of plant nutrients.

◆ pH affects the cation-exchange capacity of clay minerals.

◆ The availability of plant nutrients depends upon the pH and oxygen content of the soil.

Questions

1 a Give **three** differences between the 2:1 and 1:1 layer silicates found in clays.
  b Predict the effect of substituting Si^{4+} by Al^{3+} in such silicates.

2 Explain how soils become acidic and why this is a disadvantage. Discuss the chemistry involved in treating such an acidic soil in order to obtain the best conditions for the availability of nutrients to plants.

CHAPTER 4

Treatment of waste

By the end of this chapter you should be able to:

1 discuss the changing composition of solid domestic waste, particularly the increased use and disposal of plastics;

2 describe the process of landfill and discuss the correct management of landfill sites;

3 outline the advantages and drawbacks of incineration as a method for disposal of solid waste.

Solid domestic waste

The average person in Western society produces roughly 2 kg of solid waste per day in their dustbins for municipal disposal. Composition obviously varies according to local characteristics, but approximate average figures for the EU in 1997 are given in *table 4.1*.

The approximate average chemical composition of solid waste is water 28%, carbon 25%, oxygen 21%, hydrogen 4%, others (for example chlorine, nitrogen, sulphur, metals) 22%.

A comparison of *table 4.1* with *table 4.2*, which was compiled 24 years earlier, shows how the composition of solid domestic waste has changed. There has been a huge growth in the use of packaging materials, particularly of plastic. Almost one-third of household waste is made up of discarded packaging material and one-third of all the plastics manufactured are used for packaging. Such plastics are PET (polyethene terephthalate), used for disposable plastic bottles, PVC (polychloroethene), used for flexible packaging, and PE (polyethene), used for carrier bags.

The main disposal methods are dumping and landfill, incineration, with or without energy recovery (see page 54), conversion to fuel and recycling. *Table 4.3* shows the ways in which domestic solid waste was treated in the UK in 1997.

Figures published in 1998 show that only 6.6% by mass of domestic waste is recycled. For plastic waste the figure drops to 2.2%. In the EU as a whole the percentage of solid domestic waste which is incinerated is twice that in the UK.

Material	Percentage composition by dry weight
paper products	39
plastics	10
glass	9
metals	7
food	19
other	16

● **Table 4.1** Composition of municipal waste; EU, 1997.

Material	Percentage composition by dry weight
paper	55
food	14
glass	9
metals	
– ferrous	7
– non-ferrous	2
garden refuse	5
wood	4
plastic	1
other (for example ash)	3

● **Table 4.2** Composition of municipal waste, 1973.

Treatment	Quantity (million tonnes)
landfill	19.6
incineration with energy recovery	1.4
incineration without energy recovery	0.6
refuse-derived fuel	0.1
recycled	1.8

● **Table 4.3** Treatment of solid domestic waste; UK, 1997.

Landfill

Landfill sites (*figure 4.1*) require frequent compacting and covering with soil to encourage decomposition of organic material by bacteria. Initial decomposition is aerobic with an accompanying increase in temperature, but when the oxygen is used up the decomposition becomes anaerobic. The gases methane, hydrogen sulphide, carbon dioxide and hydrogen are produced and need to be vented (allowed to escape into the atmosphere). Sometimes the vented methane is collected and used as a fuel. There have been cases reported where hydrogen sulphide released from landfill sites has accumulated in the cabs of vehicles working at the site, with dangerous effects on the drivers of the vehicles.

Correct management of landfill sites is important. Organic acids are produced in the decomposition process and these, when leached out with rain-water, can transport heavy metals. Poor management can lead to high concentrations in the leach-water. This can continue for some considerable time after closure of the site. Species which tend to concentrate in the leach-water from landfills are chlorine, iron, manganese, zinc and nitrate.

To prevent leach-water from contaminating ground-water, an elaborate collection system is usually installed before any solid waste is tipped into the site. One of the criteria considered when a site is chosen is the ability of the material forming the base of the site to allow water to seep through it. A site is usually chosen where the base material is clay, as this will not allow water to pass through it easily. The clay is covered with a watertight liner on top of which is constructed a system of stones and perforated pipes which will drain off the leach-water.

There can be an accumulation of hazardous substances in the soil surrounding a landfill site, leading to contamination and an accumulation of toxins in the food chain.

When tipping on a site has ceased, it is covered to prevent surface water getting in, soil is placed on top and grass sown, in order to return the site as near as possible to its original condition.

The use of landfill to dispose of solid waste is now being strongly discouraged in the UK by both the lack of available new sites and the imposition of taxes.

● **Figure 4.1** Landfill sites can offer the cheapest means of disposing of municipal wastes, although this is less true with new landfill taxes.

Biodegradable plastics

The increasing use of plastics adds to the problems of landfill management because plastics take a very long time to decompose. To help deal with this problem, more biodegradable plastics are now being used because they are broken down more easily.

■ **Biopolymers** are polymers which are produced naturally. An example is PHB, poly(3-hydroxybutanoic acid). PHB is made from glucose by certain bacteria and is used by the bacteria as a source of energy. Microorganisms in soil, and in landfill sites, can break PHB down within 9 months. The properties of PHB can be modified to suit a particular use by co-polymerising it with other polymers. Unfortunately, biopolymers are several times more expensive to produce than conventional polymers.

SAQ 4.1

Draw the repeating unit of PHB. What is the functional group which joins the units together?

There are also synthetic plastics which are designed to be biodegradable. Some items made from poly(ethene) have starch incorporated into them. When the item is buried microorganisms digest the starch and the item breaks into very small pieces which can degrade more quickly.

- **Dissolving plastics** have been produced using poly(ethenol):

$$-CH_2-CH-CH_2-CH-$$
$$\quad\quad\ \ |\quad\quad\quad\ \ |$$
$$\quad\quad OH\quad\quad\ OH$$

By adjusting the number of hydroxy groups, this polymer can be designed to be soluble in cold water, warm water or only hot water.

- **Photodegradable plastics** are designed to break down in sunlight. Carbonyl groups are incorporated into the polymer chain by polymerising the monomer with carbon monoxide, CO. The carbonyl group absorbs radiation in the near-ultraviolet (270–360 nm). The energy absorbed breaks nearby bonds in the carbon chain and causes the polymer to break up. Needless to say, this type of plastic would not degrade in a landfill site – unless it was on the surface!

Incineration

Incineration (*figure 4.2*) greatly reduces the bulk of solid waste, producing an ash of much more

- **Figure 4.2** Incineration plant at Renfrewshire, Scotland.

uniform composition. The problem with incineration is air pollution. For complete combustion, a temperature of 800–1000 °C is required. Around 800 kg of waste gases are produced per tonne of refuse burnt. Most of this is carbon dioxide, a 'greenhouse gas' (see chapter 1, page 23).

Other gases produced during incineration are sulphur dioxide, SO_2, nitrogen oxides, NO_x, hydrogen chloride, HCl, hydrogen fluoride, HF, carbon monoxide, CO, and dinitrogen oxide, N_2O. Toxic gases must be removed from the exhaust gases before they are emitted into the atmosphere. Typical incineration products are shown in *table 4.4*. Approximately three times the quantity of air needed for incineration is introduced into the incinerator, hence the figures given in *table 4.4* include the oxygen and nitrogen from this air.

Product	Amount of gas by volume (%)
nitrogen	79.6
oxygen	14.3
carbon dioxide	6.0
carbon monoxide	0.06
hydrogen chloride	0.005–0.05
nitrogen oxides	0.0093
sulphur dioxide	0.0022

- **Table 4.4** Incineration products of municipal waste.

Water vapour (640 kg per tonne of refuse) and solid residues (220 kg per tonne of refuse) are also produced.

As shown in *table 4.1*, about 10% by mass of domestic waste is plastic material. This plastic material can be put to good use in the incineration of solid waste as it releases a lot of energy when it burns, which will help consume other less combustible domestic refuse. Incineration of plastics produces carbon dioxide, water, carbon monoxide and nitrogen oxides. Poly(chloroethene), PVC, also produces hydrogen chloride, while poly(propenenitrile) produces a certain amount of hydrogen cyanide.

Heating in the absence of air (pyrolysis) at 850–1050 °C reduces the amount of these gaseous pollutants that is produced, giving a mixture composed of 54% hydrogen, 25% carbon dioxide, 10% carbon monoxide and 10% methane, together with traces of nitrogen, hydrogen chloride and ammonia. The combustible gases produced (hydrogen, carbon monoxide and methane) can be used for heating.

It is important to control the temperature of incineration, since at higher temperatures highly toxic dioxins and dibenzofurans (*figure 4.3*) may be produced from rubbish containing PVC and aromatic compounds. Dioxins can become widely dispersed in the environment as a consequence of their highly stable structure and slow rate of degradation. Dioxins are extremely toxic and can cause skin, liver and kidney diseases, cancer and birth defects.

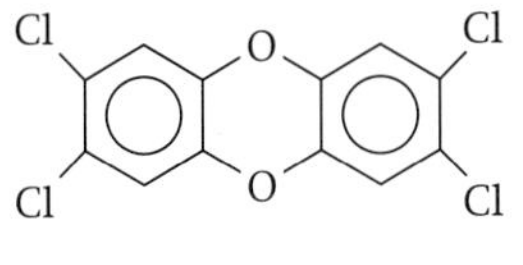

a dioxin

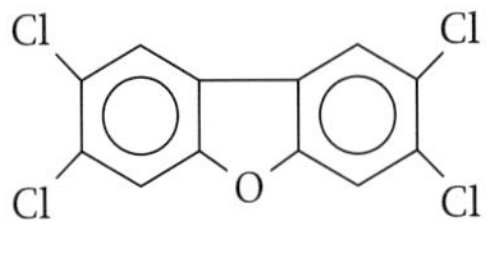

a dibenzofuran

● **Figure 4.3** General formulae of dioxins and dibenzofurans.

SAQ 4.2

What are the advantages and disadvantages of incineration as compared to landfill as a method for disposal of plastics?

SUMMARY

- Increased use of packaging materials, particularly plastics, presents problems in the disposal of solid domestic waste.

- Suitable landfill sites are becoming difficult to find, more expensive to use and, if not managed properly, can give rise to poisonous gases and contamination of soil and ground-water.

- Incineration of domestic solid waste reduces its bulk considerably. Incineration plants are expensive to build and can lead to air pollution with highly toxic substances unless carefully controlled.

Questions

1 A sanitary landfill is a means of waste handling that is much less disruptive to the environment than uncontrolled dumping either on land or in the ocean.
Describe how such a landfill should be managed and mention particularly the chemical problems associated with such a waste handling scheme.

2 Incineration is a means of disposing of municipal waste that is being used increasingly in some countries.
Discuss the advantages and disadvantages of this means of disposal.

Answers to self-assessment questions

Chapter 1

1.1 In winter there is less photosynthesis due to the lower temperature, less sunlight and the loss of leaves from deciduous plants. As a result, less carbon dioxide is removed from the atmosphere by photosynthesis. At the same time, more fossil fuels are burnt to keep us warm, putting more carbon dioxide into the atmosphere. Thus carbon dioxide levels are increased in winter.

At night, plant respiration takes place, releasing carbon dioxide, but there is virtually no photosynthesis to remove carbon dioxide. Thus the carbon dioxide level increases.

1.2 Chlorophyll absorbs at 660–680 nm (red) and 425–430 nm (blue) and reflects in the green area.

1.3 By providing an increased carbon dioxide concentration and a damp atmosphere, together with a temperature of about 15–20 °C and artificial radiation of about 680 nm and 430 nm.

1.4 Photosynthesis is rapid in rainforests. This removes excess carbon dioxide from the atmosphere and helps maintain a balance. Removal of rainforests will lead to an increase in atmospheric carbon dioxide and hence global warming.

1.5 Reactions following the absorption of radiation are exothermic, for example:

$$O^* + O_2 + M \longrightarrow O_3 + M^*; \qquad \Delta H = -100 \, \text{kJ mol}^{-1}$$
$$O_3 + O^* \longrightarrow 2O_2; \qquad \Delta H = -390 \, \text{kJ mol}^{-1}$$
$$H\cdot + O_3 \longrightarrow HO\cdot + O_2; \qquad \Delta H = -326 \, \text{kJ mol}^{-1}$$

Radiation is more intense at a greater height. Therefore, as these exothermic reactions are preceded by reactions that absorb radiation (*reactions 1.10* and *1.12*), more reactions will take place with increasing height and temperature will rise.

1.6 **a** Production:

$$O_2 \overset{hf}{\longrightarrow} O + O^*$$
$$O^* + O_2 + M \longrightarrow O_3 + M^*$$

b Removal:

$$O_3 \overset{hf}{\longrightarrow} O_2 + O$$
$$O_3 + O^* \longrightarrow 2O_2$$
$$NO\cdot + O_3 \longrightarrow NO_2\cdot + O_2$$
$$H\cdot + O_3 \longrightarrow HO\cdot + O_2$$

1.7 Lack of reactivity.

1.8

$$CCl_2F_2 \overset{hf}{\longrightarrow} \cdot CClF_2 + Cl\cdot$$
$$Cl\cdot + O_3 \longrightarrow ClO\cdot + O_2$$
$$ClO\cdot + NO\cdot \longrightarrow Cl\cdot + NO_2\cdot$$
$$ClO\cdot + NO_2\cdot \longrightarrow ClNO_2 + O$$
$$ClO\cdot + O \longrightarrow Cl\cdot + O_2$$

1.9 Hydrofluorocarbons (HFCs) and hydrochlorofluorocarbons (HCFCs) are now being used as substitutes for CFCs. They contain C–H bonds which are broken down in the troposphere. This initiates breakdown of the entire molecule and the chlorine is thus unable to reach the stratosphere. Their disadvantage is that they are potent greenhouse gases.

1.10 Nitrogen monoxide is emitted from cars in the morning rush hour. At first this is slowly oxidised to nitrogen dioxide *(reaction 1.48)*, the concentration of which peaks about two hours later than that of nitrogen monoxide because of the absence of an effective oxidising agent. Full daylight splits up nitrogen dioxide, releasing oxygen atoms *(1.50)*. These react with oxygen molecules in the presence of particulate matter from car exhausts to form ozone *(1.51)*, which builds to a peak concentration in the early afternoon. Nitrogen monoxide formed later in the day removes the ozone to re-form oxygen molecules *(1.52)*. The nitrogen dioxide formed does not undergo further photolysis as there is little light in the evening rush hour.

1.11 2-methylbuta-1,3-diene.

1.12 **a** A secondary pollutant is one which is formed by the chemical reactions of emitted pollutants.

b Emission of nitrogen oxides and particulates to be restricted by the use of catalytic converters in motor vehicles and a higher air : fuel ratio to ensure more complete combustion. Smoke emission can be stopped or electrostatic precipitators can be used to eliminate it.

1.13 For petrol vehicles:
HC and NO_x emissions in 1992
   $= 0.97\,g$ per kilometre
HC and NO_x emissions in 2005
   $= 0.18\,g$ per kilometre
reduction $= 0.79\,g$ per kilometre

CO emissions in 1992 $= 2.72\,g$ per kilometre
CO emissions in 2005 $= 1.00\,g$ per kilometre
reduction $= 1.72\,g$ per kilometre

For diesel vehicles:
HC and NO_x emissions in 1992
   $= 0.97\,g$ per kilometre
HC and NO_x emissions in 2005
   $= 0.30\,g$ per kilometre
reduction $= 0.67\,g$ per kilometre

CO emissions in 1992 $= 2.72\,g$ per kilometre
CO emissions in 2005 $= 0.50\,g$ per kilometre
reduction $= 2.22\,g$ per kilometre

1.14 13 billion tonnes more carbon equivalent burnt. This will produce $13 \times \frac{44}{12} = 47.7$ billion tonnes of carbon dioxide, assuming complete combustion.

1.15 A considerable amount of the carbon dioxide released into the troposphere dissolves in the oceans and is removed by phytoplankton or reacts with the water. Cold water in northern oceans sinks to great depths, taking the dissolved carbon dioxide with it. Thus the oceans effectively act as a sink for the removal of some of the carbon dioxide in the atmosphere.

Chapter 2

2.1 Carbon dioxide dissolves in rain-water, and some of the dissolved carbon dioxide reacts with the water to form aqueous hydrogen ions ($H^+(aq)$):
$$CO_2(g) \rightleftharpoons CO_2(aq)$$
$$CO_2(aq) + H_2O(l) \rightleftharpoons H^+(aq) + HCO_3^-(aq)$$
$$HCO_3^-(aq) \rightleftharpoons H^+(aq) + CO_3^{2-}(aq)$$

The natural acidity of rain-water is enhanced when sulphur oxides and nitrogen oxides dissolve in the rain:
$$SO_2(g) + H_2O(l) \rightleftharpoons H_2SO_3(aq)$$
$$H_2SO_3(aq) \rightleftharpoons H^+(aq) + HSO_3^-(aq)$$
$$HSO_3^-(aq) \rightleftharpoons H^+(aq) + SO_3^{2-}(aq)$$
The $HSO_3^-(aq)$ in the water droplets can be oxidised:
$$HSO_3^-(aq) + H_2O(l) \longrightarrow HSO_4^-(aq) + 2H^+(aq) + 2e^-$$
$$3NO_2{}^\bullet(g) + H_2O(l) \longrightarrow 2HNO_3(aq) + NO^\bullet(g)$$
Acid rain destroys aquatic life, leaches nutrients from the soil, enables toxic metal ions to dissolve in soil solution and so enter the food chain, leads to corrosion of metals and buildings and affects the growth of trees.

2.2 Dissolved oxygen is essential for respiration by aquatic life and for the decomposition of organic material:
$$[CH_2O](aq) + O_2(g) \xrightarrow{\text{microorganisms}} CO_2(g) + H_2O(l)$$
The level of dissolved oxygen decreases rapidly immediately downstream from introduction of the pollutant due to the oxidation of organic material. For a while it remains low, then it starts to increase as increasing levels of sunlight penetrate the water, until the original level is restored.

2.3 Too many nutrients in lakes and rivers, particularly phosphate and nitrate, cause excessive growth of algae and plants. When these plants die and decompose they use up dissolved oxygen from the water. Eventually the oxygen supply becomes so low that fish and other aquatic animals die. The decomposed remains from the algae give off foul-smelling substances.

2.4 $Ca^{2+}(aq)$ and $Mg^{2+}(aq)$
Dissolved carbon dioxide makes water weakly acidic. This acidic water reacts with limestone, forming calcium ions in aqueous solution.

In the process of ion exchange, hard water is passed through resins which exchange hydrogen or sodium ions for calcium and magnesium ions:
$$2resin^-H^+(s) + Ca^{2+}(aq)$$
$$\longrightarrow (resin^-)_2Ca^{2+}(s) + 2H^+(aq)$$
$$2resin^-Na^+(s) + Ca^{2+}(aq)$$
$$\longrightarrow (resin^-)_2Ca^{2+}(s) + 2Na^+(aq)$$
Thus the calcium and magnesium ions are removed from the water.

Chapter 3

3.1 *Reaction 3.9*
sulphur: −1 to +6
Reaction 3.10
iron: +2 to +3

3.2 **a** Mn: +2 to +4
O_2: 0 to −2
   b Mn: +2 to +4
O_2: 0 to −2
   c S: −2 to +6
O_2: 0 to −2

3.3

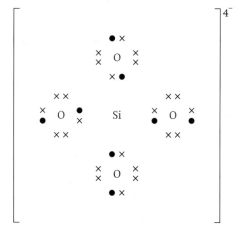

3.4 The aluminium ion, Al^{3+}, has a high charge density. It neutralises the negative charges on the surfaces of the layers of clay particles, and this breaks up the layer structure to form a precipitate.

3.5 As plants remove nutrients from the water in the soil, equilibria such as *reaction 3.17* move to the right to release more of the nutrient to the soil solution.

3.6 At low pH hydrogen ions will displace the nutrient cation from the surface of the clay:
clay–K(s) + H^+(aq) $\rightleftharpoons$ clay–H(s) + K^+(aq)
The nutrient cation can then be leached out of the soil.

At high pH the hydroxyl groups on the surface of clays lose protons, or the protons are replaced by cationic nutrients – see reactions 3.14 and 3.15. This increases surface cation-exchange capacity. However, some cationic nutrients may be precipitated at high pH – see table 3.5.

3.7 A well-aerated soil will ensure iron is maintained in its most highly oxidised form of iron(III). A pH not above 6 will ensure the maximum availability of iron(III); above this pH the iron is precipitated as iron(III) hydroxide.

Nitrate(V) is prevented from being reduced to ammonium ions by a well-aerated soil and a high pH – see *reaction 3.23*.

Maximum availability of phosphate is at a pH of between 6 and 8 – see *table 3.5*.

Thus to ensure a good supply of all three of the above nutrients, a pH of 6 and a well-aerated soil should be provided.

3.8 Kaolinite has the lowest buffering capacity and montmorillonite the highest. Kaolinite, being a 1:1 clay with hydrogen bonding between the layers, has the lowest surface area per unit mass and therefore has fewest ions per unit mass on its surface to buffer the effect of the added hydroxide ions.

Chapter 4

4.1

$$\left[O-\overset{\displaystyle CH_3}{\underset{\displaystyle |}{CH}}-CH_2-\overset{\displaystyle O}{\underset{\displaystyle ||}{C}} \right]_n$$

The units are joined together by an ester linkage. PHB is a polyester.

4.2 Advantages of incineration:
- considerably reduced bulk of solid waste;
- ash produced is of a uniform composition;
- plastics release a lot of energy when they burn, which helps consume less combustible refuse.

Disadvantages of incineration:
- increases emission of carbon dioxide to the atmosphere;
- produces toxic gases, such as carbon monoxide, hydrogen chloride and hydrogen cyanide, which have to be removed from the exhaust gases – this is expensive;
- releases nitrogen oxides to the atmosphere, which can then become involved in photochemical smog and acid rain;
- dioxins and dibenzofurans may be synthesised at high temperatures – these are highly toxic.

Glossary

aerobic decomposition Decomposition, brought about by bacteria, when there is a plentiful supply of oxygen.

anaerobic decomposition Decomposition when there is insufficient oxygen for aerobic decomposition.

carbon cycle A natural cycle which interchanges carbon between the Earth's surface and the troposphere, thus maintaining a relatively constant concentration of carbon dioxide in the troposphere.

catalytic converter A device fitted to the exhaust system of petrol and diesel engines which reduces the emission of pollutants by the use of heterogeneous catalysts.

cation exchange Interchange of cationic nutrients between the surface of a clay and the surrounding soil solution.

colloids Very small particles (1–100 nm) dispersed in a liquid or gaseous medium and not separating out.

global warming The increase in average temperature of the Earth's surface caused by an enhanced **greenhouse effect** due to increased concentration of greenhouse gases (e.g. carbon dioxide) in the atmosphere.

greenhouse effect Natural phenomenon by which some gases present in the atmosphere absorb infrared radiation emitted from the Earth's surface and then re-emit some of this infrared radiation back to the Earth's surface.

hardness of water The difficulty in producing a good lather with soap and the 'furring' of heating elements due to the presence of calcium and magnesium ions in the water.

photochemical reactions Reactions which are brought about by the action of electromagnetic radiation on matter.

photochemical smog A whitish yellow haze containing nitrogen oxides, hydrocarbons, peroxy compounds, ozone and aldehydes, produced by the action of sunlight on nitrogen oxides and hydrocarbons in the troposphere.

potable water Water which is deemed to be 'drinkable' and can be consumed without harm to the user.

radicals Reactive atoms or molecules with an unpaired electron. *Formerly* **free radicals**.

residence time The average length of time a given pollutant remains in the atmosphere.

stratosphere The region of the atmosphere that extends from 10–16 km to 60 km above the Earth's surface.

temperature inversion A situation in which temperature increases with height above the Earth's surface until a certain height when the trend then changes to the normal decrease in temperature with height. This traps a layer of cold air under warmer air.

temporary hardness The type of **hardness of water** that can be removed by boiling.

troposphere The region of the atmosphere that extends from the Earth's surface to a height of 10–16 km.

weathering The breaking down of rocks and rock surfaces by the action of water, oxygen and carbon dioxide.

Bibliography

Bond R. G. and Straub C. P., *Handbook of Environmental Control*, CRC Press, Cleveland, OH, USA.

Digest of Environmental Statistics, No. 20, HMSO, London.

Europe's Environment, European Environment Agency, Copenhagen.

Fergusson J. E., *Inorganic Chemistry and the Earth*, Pergamon Press, Oxford.

Finlayson-Pitts B. J. and Pitts J. N. Jnr, *Atmospheric Chemistry*, John Wiley, Chichester.

Harrison R. N., ed., *Understanding our Environment*, Royal Society of Chemistry, Cambridge.

Purves D., *Trace Element Contamination of the Environment*, Elsevier, Amsterdam.

Pollution, Royal Society of Chemistry, Cambridge.

United Nations Environment Project website, http://www.unep.ch/

Index

Terms shown in **bold** also appear in the glossary (see page 59).
Pages in *italics* refer to figures.